E-Learning in the 21st Century

There is currently a technological revolution taking place in higher education. The growth of e-learning is being described as explosive, unprecedented, and above all, disruptive. This timely and comprehensive book provides a coherent framework for understanding e-learning in higher education.

The authors draw on their extensive research in the area to explore the technological, pedagogical and organizational implications of e-learning, and more importantly, they provide practical models for educators to use to realize the full potential of e-learning. A unique feature of the book is that the authors focus less on the specifics of the ever-evolving technologies and more on the search for an understanding of these technologies from an educational perspective.

This book will be invaluable for researchers, practitioners and senior administrators looking for guidance on how to successfully adopt e-learning in their institutions. It will also appeal to anyone with an interest in the impact of e-learning on higher education and society.

D. R. Garrison is the Director of the Learning Commons and Professor in the Faculty of Education at the University of Calgary, Canada. He was formerly a Professor and Dean at the Faculty of Extension at the University of Alberta. Dr Garrison's areas of research relate to the teaching and learning transaction in the context of adult distance and higher education.

Terry Anderson is Professor and Research Chair in Distance Education at Athabasca University, Canada. He was the former Director of the Academic Technologies for Learning at the University of Alberta. Terry has 15 years of experience related to distance education as a teacher, researcher and administrator, including employment as Director of Contact North in Northern Ontario.

E-Learning in the 21st Century

A Framework for Research and Practice

D. R. Garrison and
Terry Anderson

RoutledgeFalmer
Taylor & Francis Group

LONDON AND NEW YORK

First published 2003
by RoutledgeFalmer
11 New Fetter Lane, London EC4P 4EE

Simultaneously published in the USA and Canada
by RoutledgeFalmer
29 West 35th Street, New York, NY 10001

Reprinted 2003 (twice), 2004 (twice)

RoutledgeFalmer is an imprint of the Taylor & Francis Group

© 2003 D. R. Garrison and Terry Anderson

Typeset in Sabon by
Keystroke, Jacaranda Lodge, Wolverhampton
Printed and bound in Great Britain by
MPG Books Ltd, Bodmin

British Library Cataloguing in Publication Data
A catalogue record for this book is available from the British Library

Library of Congress Cataloging in Publication Data
A catalog record for this book has been requested

ISBN 0–415–26346–8 (pbk)
ISBN 0–415–26345–X (hbk)

Contents

Illustrations

FIGURES

TABLES

Preface

The goal of 'e-learning in the twenty-first century' is to provide a framework for understanding the application of e-learning in higher education. We view e-learning as that learning facilitated on-line through network technologies. This does not preclude any number of other technologies or approaches, including compoents of face-to-face educational experiences. However, we will confine our discussion to those learning activities conducted through electronic means on-line.

Various authors have described the growth of e-learning as explosive, unprecedented, amazing, and disruptive. In fact, there are those who argue that we are experiencing a revolution in higher education (University of Illinois 1999). Others suggest that e-learning technology is unique (Harasim 1989) and represents a new era of distance education (Garrison 1997a). Regardless of the rhetoric, what has changed is the 'speed and power of communications and the expanded capacity to send, receive, and use information' (Ikenberry 1999: 57) and the capacity to bridge time and space for educational purposes.

While lifelong learning has become an imperative, and communications technologies are transforming higher education, in most instances 'the revolution proceeds without any clear vision or master plan' (Ikenberry 1999: 58). Considering the massive adoption of e-learning, what is surprising, and cause for concern, is that we know so little about the use of this medium to facilitate learning (Gilbert 2000). To date, published research and guides consist of innumerable case studies and personal descriptions and prescriptions but little in the way of rigorous, research-based constructs that lead to an in-depth understanding of e-learning in higher education.

Considering the ubiquity of e-learning, and the enormous opportunities and risks that it presents for higher education, we need more than a fragmented approach to studying and understanding this phenomenon. Is e-learning to be used simply to enhance inherently deficient existing practices (e.g., lecturing)? Or does this technology have the potential to transform the educational transaction towards the ideal of a community of inquiry (Garrison and Anderson 2000)? Such questions can only be addressed and explored through empirically based research frameworks such as those presented in this book.

HOW THE BOOK CAME TO BE

The authors will provide educators with a deep understanding of the characteristics of e-learning. This in-depth understanding will give direction and guidance to educators who wish to facilitate critical discourse and higher-order learning through the use of electronic technologies in a networked learning context. All universities and colleges now have large numbers of faculty members using e-learning to enhance their campus-based and distance-education programming. Some of the most innovative technological e-learning approaches are being built in corporations to improve performance and retain competitive advantages.

OVERVIEW OF CONTENTS

The first chapter describes the context and outlines the challenges of exploring and understanding the potential of e-learning. It makes the point that e-learning is not just another learning technology. There is every reason to believe it will transform teaching and learning.

The second chapter outlines the philosophical perspective and theoretical concepts that frame our understanding of e-learning. It also outlines a set of principles that guide a deep and meaningful approach to e-learning.

The third chapter speaks to the organizing concept for realizing the potential of e-learning. The community of inquiry model is the conceptual framework that defines the three constituting elements of e-learning – social, cognitive, and teaching presence. This conceptual model takes us back to the roots and core values of higher education. We then discuss the place of technology in this learning community.

The fourth chapter provides an overview of technology and its development. The impact of the Internet as well as the role and nature of interaction in e-learning is then discussed.

The fifth chapter explores the challenge of creating a climate for higher-order learning in an e-learning environment. Categories, indicators, and suggestions that have practical value in establishing social presence are provided.

The sixth chapter offers an analysis and model of critical thinking and practical inquiry for cognitive presence. From this, descriptors and indicators for each of the phases of practical inquiry are described. This provides insights into the cognitive dimensions of e-learning.

The seventh chapter completes the community of inquiry model with a discussion of teaching presence and its central function in e-learning. Categories and indicators of teaching presence are outlined and practical implications for structuring, facilitating, and directing are addressed.

The eighth chapter shifts to the practical issues of implementing e-learning. It begins by discussing the purposes and strengths of various learning activities. The rest of the chapter approaches e-learning from the perspective of teaching presence and its dimensions but focusing on issues of social and cognitive presence. Guidelines and specific suggestions for practice are provided.

The ninth chapter addresses assessment and evaluation that is arguably the most influential element of any educational experience. Assessment of e-learning goes beyond judging student performance. Assessment of the development and delivery of e-learning is also necessary to advance our understanding of meaningful and worthwhile learning.

The tenth chapter moves out of the classroom to consider institutional issues to prepare for e-learning in the twenty-first century. The chapter explores the dynamics of change and the need for leadership, policy, and infrastructure with regard to innovation and the strategic integration of e-learning in institutions of higher education.

The last chapter provides an imaginative look into the future with regard to e-learning. Its unique properties are described and a glimpse into the future provided.

CONTRIBUTION

The early chapters demonstrate that e-learning can create asynchronous communities of inquiry which have the potential to support the development of collaborative communities of learning, while still allowing 'anytime–anywhere' access by students. We are convinced that such technology, when combined with effective pedagogy and reflective teaching, will transform higher education. In the later chapters of the book, this potential is translated into practical guidelines intended to be used by educators working to realize the full potential of e-learning.

This book contributes a meaningful framework and approach to the understanding of the fundamentals of e-learning and explains why it is proliferating throughout a rapidly evolving learning society. This is the first comprehensive and coherent framework to guide our understanding of e-learning in higher education and society.

To this point, communications technologies have been driving the unprecedented growth of e-learning. The focus in this book is less on the specifics of the ever-evolving technologies used for e-learning, and more on the search for a deep understanding of these technologies from an educational perspective. It is to the purpose of mapping the territory of e-learning, then providing directional choices for higher education and specific guidelines to reach worthwhile destinations, that this book makes its contribution.

This book is of particular relevance to those who are less impressed with technological gadgetry but who have been waiting for a strong pedagogical reason to participate in the paradigm shift in teaching and learning that e-learning represents. This book will appeal to a broad audience interested in e-learning. The primary audiences, however, are researchers, practitioners, and senior administrators in higher education who must guide the adoption in their institutions of this unique and rapidly proliferating technology.

This book can be used as a basic research framework and tool to study and understand the characteristics of e-learning and to explore its optimal educational applications. It will also be useful as a text-book for adult education and training as well as any number of instructional-technology and distance-education courses. Finally, it will be a valuable reference and guide for senior decision-makers in higher education.

Acknowledgements

We would like to acknowledge the contributions of Walter Archer who was our co-investigator during the research that provided the foundation for this book. Unfortunately, Dr Archer was unable to continue our collaboration due to the demands of a new decanal position. We also wish to acknowledge the contributions of Liam Rourke, our research assistant for the three years of the project, and who contributed far beyond that of a graduate research assistant. His contributions are particularly evident in the methodology paper in Appendix B.

Finally, we wish to acknowledge a grant from the Social Sciences and Humanities Research Council of Canada which supported the original study that was the catalyst for this book.

Chapter 1

Introduction

> When some people look at a room full of desks facing a central podium,
> they see a dinosaur.
>
> (Young 1997)

> There is no progress . . . in how we teach, despite what might be
> possible with the new technology.
>
> (Laurillard 2002: 20)

It has been argued that computer-based communication is the most
fundamental change in communications technology in the last 150 years
(de la Sola Pool 1984). The proliferation of the personal computer combined
with the Internet has precipitated far-reaching changes in society. Electronic
communications and digital networks are transforming the way we work
and are reshaping personal communication and entertainment. This transformation has had a tremendous effect on the need and opportunity to learn.
Unfortunately, the transmission model that still dominates education has
changed little.

Notwithstanding the widespread adoption of computer communications
in society, we have yet to fully experience the transformative effects of this
medium, particularly its effect on e-learning. We are in what John Seely
Brown (2000) described as the gradual development phase of this transformative medium and are yet to experience its explosive impact. We are
only experiencing e-learning in its early forms and have much to learn of its
inherent capabilities and the creation of a new 'learning ecology' (Brown
2000). What are e-learning's relative advantages and are they compelling
enough to force a reconceptualization of the teaching and learning
transaction? Perhaps, because of our inability to come to grips with this new
learning ecology, education is largely unchanged by communication
technology that has transformed society in many other ways.

As has been suggested, e-learning is not simply another technology or add-
on that will be quietly integrated or ultimately rejected. As discussed in
subsequent chapters, e-learning represents a very different category and mode

of communication. Since communication is at the heart of all forms of educational interaction, it is likely that its impact on education systems and individual teachers and learners will be significant. It makes little sense to replicate or simulate traditional face-to-face approaches. Clearly, if we really are experiencing a new learning ecology, simulating practices based on a very different ecology simply misses the point. Not only would opportunities to improve the learning experience be lost, but merely simulating traditional practices resists capitalizing on the characteristics of a new era of learning.

E-learning will inevitably transform all forms of education and learning in the twenty-first century. Notwithstanding that e-learning's influence in traditional educational institutions has been weak – in reality, little more than an enhancement of current practices – as we gain a better understanding of its potential and strengths, e-learning will effectively transform how we approach the teaching and learning transaction (Garrison and Anderson 2000). E-learning transforms education in ways that extend beyond the efficient delivery or entertainment value of traditional approaches. E-learning cannot be ignored by those who are seriously committed to enhancing teaching and learning.

This book will provide the foundational understanding of e-learning while it investigates its unique potential to support constructive communities of inquiry consistent with the long-held ideals of higher education. We will provide a coherent perspective and use the term e-learning in an inclusive manner. Broadly defined, e-learning is networked, on-line learning that takes place in a formal context and uses a range of multimedia technologies. Within that broad parameter, we will focus on the dominant educational feature of this technology to support asynchronous, collaborative learning.

A NEW REALITY

At the core of the e-learning transformation is the Internet. A report of the US Web-based Education Commission (on-line) stated:

> The question is no longer if the Internet can be used to transform learning in new and powerful ways. The Commission has found that it can. The Web-based Education Commission calls upon the new Congress and Administration to embrace an 'e-learning' agenda as a centrepiece of our nation's federal education policy.
>
> (Retrieved July 2001)

The report recommended that a vastly expanded development and innovation programme 'should be built on a deeper understanding of how people learn, how new tools support and assess learning gains, what kinds of organizational structures support these gains, and what is needed to keep the field of learning moving forward.'

Similarly, the Advisory Committee for Online Learning stated that the focus 'must be the quality of the learning experience' (2000: 28) and care and understanding is required to ensure such experiences. Moreover, it suggested that the potential of e-learning is clear and that we ignore it at our peril. Creating an e-learning experience involves 'a serious commitment to understanding the very different features of this medium and the ways it can be used most advantageously to impart learning' (p. 52).

E-learning is an open system. With the power of the Internet, the teaching and learning transaction is exposed to unfathomable amounts of information. This exposure is a tremendously powerful attraction to teachers and learners; however, its engagement may not always be effective nor efficient. Openness offers conservative forces and narrow views unfettered access to differing perspectives and ideas. However, there must also be limiting and stabilizing influences if e-learning is to maintain a sense of community and purpose, not to mention sustainability.

The essential feature of e-learning extends beyond its access to information and builds on its communicative and interactive features. The goal of quality e-learning is to blend diversity and cohesiveness into a dynamic and intellectually challenging 'learning ecology.' This interactivity goes far beyond the one-way transmission of content and extends our thinking regarding communications among human beings engaged in the educational process.

Not long ago, the provision of increased learner independence in terms of space and time meant a corresponding loss of collaboration and increased isolation. Independence and collaboration seemed contradictions. More of one inherently meant less of the other. The transformational power of e-learning goes to the heart of this issue. We now can provide freedom and control within a vibrant community of inquiry. E-learning recognizes and integrates the personal and public aspects of an educational experience. This will be more fully explored in subsequent chapters related to collaborative constructive learning and critical reflection and discourse (practical inquiry).

To realize the potential of e-learning as an open but cohesive system, it is essential that we rethink our pedagogy. Education is about ideas not facts. Moreover, students in higher education are not receiving the educational experiences they need to develop the critical and self-directed higher education skills required for lifelong learning. The learning outcomes are generally substandard in relation to the demands of the twenty-first century. With its large lecture halls and standardized, objective testing, traditional undergraduate education has taken on an industrial character. Fundamentally, lecturing is about imparting information not about encouraging critical thinking or even about understanding ideas. Access to information is not the problem. We have far greater access to information than we can manage. E-learning's transformative power and capacity to add value is not based upon access. What is required, and what e-learning offers, are better ways to process, make sense of, and recreate this information. The current passive-information-transfer approaches of higher education are contrasted with the interactive and constructive potential of e-learning.

While e-learning can support and even marginally enhance current practices, such as lecturing, the real impact will be to precipitate new approaches that recognize and seize e-learning's interactive capabilities. In reality, this may well be a back-to-the-future scenario as we return to educational experiences founded in communities of inquiry. A community where individual experiences and ideas are recognized and discussed in light of societal knowledge, norms, and values. Where autonomy and collaboration are not conflicting or contradictory terms but the essential elements of a unified and qualitative shift in the process of critical inquiry.

For e-learning to have a significant place in education it must prove that it is more than a medium to conveniently access content. Institutions of higher education have slowly begun to appreciate that the content of an educational experience alone will not define quality learning but that the context – how teachers design that experience, and the interactions that drive the learning transaction – will ultimately distinguish each institution. A quality educational experience is the dynamic integration of content and context created and facilitated by a discipline expert and pedagogically competent teacher. We express these themes in our model of practical inquiry and in the discussion of cognitive and social presence that is operationalized through teaching presence.

The asynchronous ecology of e-learning, from the perspective of the authors of this book, is that it is the context and process of e-learning that makes it unique and if we are to achieve quality education, it is context and process that must be attended to. Convenient or unlimited access to information is not the issue, notwithstanding this powerful capability. In fact, it is this over-powering capability that has at times obfuscated contextual and pedagogical concerns. Surfing the Internet, no more than wandering through a library, is not an educational experience and it is fatuous to acknowledge it as anything more than entertainment or a pleasant pastime.

At the core of the e-learning context is a collaborative constructive transaction. E-learning is exciting from this perspective in that it enhances and enriches both content and context. The challenge is to design and create a context, with appropriate levels of social presence, which is congruent with the content and the reinforcement of the educational goals that will enhance cognitive presence and the realization of higher-order learning outcomes. When the properties and powers of e-learning are recognized and applied, the depth of learning and quality of cognitive presence will not be surpassed.

MYTHS

This book challenges the myth that higher education today comprises a community of learners dedicated to achieving higher-order learning outcomes. There is far more rhetoric than reality in the assertion that communities of inquiry in higher education today encourage students to approach learning in a critical manner and process information in a deep and meaningful way.

In the mid-1980s, the personal computer became a reality in that it became accessible to a huge and growing number of people. Today, it is the essential interface to the Internet and the World Wide Web, and is transforming teaching and learning. We are just beginning to discover and understand the extent to which these technologies will transform expectations for, and approaches to, learning. These technologies do not represent more of the same. With the ubiquity of communications technologies and their multiple forms (e.g., text, visual, voice) we are in the early stages of a true paradigm shift and we have yet to experience the full effect. The application with perhaps the greatest influence on education and society is e-learning or on-line learning. In particular, it makes practicable a means of asynchronous collaborative learning, which, until recently, seemed an oxymoron in educational spheres.

The technological developments just outlined are causing educators to rethink not only how learning might be approached but, as a result of these very developments, how new learning outcomes will be both possible and necessary. Global communications within intimate learning communities will create opportunities for cross-cultural knowledge development.

The knowledge era and the accompanying new economy have recognized, and placed increased value on thinking and learning abilities. The challenge is to turn e-information into human knowledge. This is not a technological problem but a social challenge that requires an educational solution. That solution lies in the integration of meaningful educational approaches with innovative technological enablers. At the intersection of this quest is e-learning, with its ability to create rich communities of inquiry in an asynchronous, anytime, anyplace context.

Another myth is that this technology is but a means to transmit information. This simplistic approach does not consider the inherent characteristics, capabilities, or potential that e-learning, for example, has to fundamentally redefine our approach to learning. Certainly, educational design and what we have students do is of paramount importance. However, the nature of the communication options available can very much affect educational possibilities. This becomes obvious when extreme methods of distance education such as correspondence and video/audio conferencing are compared. The first generally relies on slow, asynchronous written communication, while the latter carries the capability for sustained, synchronous verbal and visual communication. E-learning supports both synchronous and asynchronous communications in multiple formats ranging from text to voice and audio. However, its compelling educational advantage is its capacity to support reflective text-based interaction, independent of the pressures of time and the constraints of distance.

Although e-learning has attracted much attention, its adoption has largely outstripped our understanding of the technology from an educational perspective. Its value is not faster access to information. The value of e-learning is in its capacity to facilitate communication and thinking and thereby construct meaning and knowledge. Upon reflection, it should be no surprise that most research into using technology for educational purposes has shown no significant differences in learning outcomes between traditional and technically advanced media. Why would we expect to find significant differences if we do essentially the same thing we always have done (both teaching and learning activities) except that the medium of communication has been changed or a deficient approach has been enhanced with some visually appealing or entertaining technology?

The assumption here is that communications technologies do have biases, or, if you wish, strengths and weaknesses. According to Chandler (1995), there is a cost with any medium as experience is enhanced or restricted, clarified or distorted, and revealed or concealed. Educators have not under-stood and capitalized on the blend of symbol systems, such as multimedia, text-based communication systems that create new modes of expression and communication. It is to the exploration and understanding of the characteristics of the medium of e-learning that we focus our attention.

> We can be so familiar with the medium that we are 'anaesthetized' to the mediation it involves: we 'don't know what we're missing'. Insofar as we are numbed to the processes involved we cannot be said to be exercising 'choices' in its use.
>
> (Chandler 1995: 10)

There can be no rational adoption of e-learning without such an appreciation of the losses and gains. Technology differentially shapes our experiences and how we see the world. E-learning is not just another tool. It will change how we experience and view learning. Exactly when the full impact of this shift will occur is not known nor is the force that will precipitate this shift to use e-learning in fundamentally new ways – ways that result in a qualitatively enhanced shift in learning process and outcomes that take us beyond access to information (i.e., 'academic shovelware') but that are more educationally grounded than the recreational, non-educational Web. In the 'too much information age' (Gilbert, 2000) we do not need greater access to information – we must learn to navigate and understand this sea of information.

That e-learning has a virtually unlimited potential to expand educational horizons is not in question. This assumption, however, is predicated upon coming to grips with the myths of higher and most other education. We are not creating engaging communities of learning committed to critical discourse and construction of deep and meaningful learning outcomes. We must first rethink our educational approaches (see next chapter) and begin to appreciate the powerful communication capabilities and potential to support the development of quality learning outcomes – not simply accessing and attempting to recall increasingly fragmented bits of information.

CONCLUSION

E-learning does not represent more of the same. Electronic communications technologies, with their multiple media text, visual, voice and their capacity to extend interaction over time and distance, are transforming teaching and learning. Notwithstanding this widespread influence and the large and growing discourse on the topic, developments in communications technology, and their adoption generally in the academy, have outpaced our understanding of how to use them to support an educational experience. The qualities that will be valued in a 'knowledge-based future' will be the ability to access and understand information. That is, the ability to order and construct knowledge. This is an enormous challenge and there are no simple rules or recipes for designing and delivering an effective e-learning experience. This is true of most educational experiences but, in the case of e-learning, is compounded by the variables and variations inherent in a deep and meaningful e-learning experience. The complexities of context and distinct communication characteristics of e-learning to support communities of inquiry do not lend themselves to easy or simplistic solutions. An e-learning experience demands the insight and agility of a reflective and knowledgeable teacher who can translate principles and guidelines to the contingencies and exigencies of their unique contexts. This necessitates critical thinking capabilities not dissimilar to those defined as goals of higher education.

In realistically addressing the complexities of e-learning, our intent is to provide conceptual order along with principles and guidelines that have generalizability and value for professional teachers. Therefore, the challenge for the reader is to make sense of the ideas presented here from their unique perspective and context. The responsibility of the educator is to understand and translate the concepts and ideas presented here and to apply them in a pragmatic manner in order to realize the specific goals and objectives of their e-learning experience.

We need to start by asking what e-learning will allow us to do that we could not do before. And how networks and interactive pedagogies can address the quality of the learning experience. This book is about doing things differently. It is not about entrenching deficient face-to-face approaches such as lecturing by using e-learning to access more incomprehensible information.

Nor is it about having students accessing the same deficient approaches through a different medium.

We find ourselves no further ahead because the regressive activities mentioned above have defined the status quo and reinforced the defensive strategy in higher education. Marshall McLuhan (1995) argued that the content of a new medium is initially always an older medium. Thus, the first use of cinema was to record plays, and the first use of the Internet was mail. Likewise, the first educational application of the Net was to disseminate lectures and replace paper syllabi. Now, however, we are challenged to go beyond these early adaptations and develop pedagogy that exploits the capacity for multimediated communications and effective storage and retrieval of very large quantities of information.

Education is but an illusion if it simply disseminates information without actively supporting a critical assessment and the opportunity to provide meaningful knowledge structures that will serve future learning challenges. The challenge is not to simply advocate or promote the use of e-learning. The real challenge and benefit is to understand the nature and potential of e-learning and its implications for how teaching and learning is, and should be, approached. E-learning is not 'infotainment.'

Increasingly, higher education is returning to its roots by focusing on the values and practices associated with collaborative approaches to learning. This is a distinct reaction to the dominant individual and isolating approaches to learning that have evolved for fiscal reasons in the last two decades of the twentieth century. Along with this is the realization that constructing personal meaning is enabled by opportunities to test one's understandings in a social context and to apply new ideas and solutions in relevant contexts. Perhaps it is time to recast the educational dinosaur and utilize the technologies of e-learning to move away from the transmission modality.

Part I

The conceptual framework

The goal of this book is to provide a framework for understanding the application of e-learning in higher education. This understanding will serve to guide both research about, and practice with, e-learning for purposes of facilitating higher-order learning. However, before we can reasonably build a coherent theoretical framework, we must make explicit the foundational values and beliefs upon which this book is based. That is the focus of the next chapter.

Chapter 2

Theoretical foundation

> Nothing has brought pedagogical theory into greater disrepute than the belief that it is identified with handing out to teachers recipes and models to be followed in teaching.
>
> (Dewey 1916: 170)

A theoretical foundation for teaching and learning will reflect fundamental values and beliefs about an educational experience. It is by making explicit the theoretical elements of an educational experience that we reveal the ideals, which we imperfectly strive to realize. When adopting new communication technologies with the potential to fundamentally alter the teaching and learning transaction, being clear as to one's ideals is particularly important. E-learning has become the protagonist for change in higher education, but the plot needs a purpose. It is to this end, to provide a clear goal upon which to construct an e-learning strategy, that we turn our attention in this chapter.

The goal of this chapter is to outline the assumptions, themes, concepts and principles that underpin the theoretical framework for e-learning described in Chapter 1. The fundamental questions addressed are associated with the nature of an educational experience and the desired learning outcomes.

PHILOSOPHICAL PERSPECTIVE

The dominant issue in education today is not access to more information. In fact, making sense of the quantity of material they are exposed to is a serious challenge for students. It is impossible to meaningfully assimilate all the information in even the narrowest of subject areas. Because of this information explosion, and the accompanying advances in communications, new approaches are required. The goal is to give students the abilities and strategies required to manage this overwhelming breadth and depth of information. In working towards this goal, educators began to realize that the only long-term solution was to construct an educational environment in which students would not only learn, but where they would learn to learn. In this regard, the focus of education is shifting to the development of critical thinking and self-directed learning abilities that can serve the individual over a lifetime. The desired outcome of education, then, becomes the construction of coherent knowledge structures that accommodate further learning, not the assimilation of specific bits of information. Ultimately, education must prepare students to be continuous learners – once the rhetoric of higher education but now the hallmark of the knowledge age.

While we believe that e-learning will most certainly be the dominant technology in supporting new approaches to teaching and learning, sound educational principles must inevitably create the foundation if we are to realize meaningful and worthwhile learning outcomes. However, before exploring specific concepts and principles, it is important to briefly explicate the educational assumptions that have shaped the framework described in subsequent chapters.

The foundational perspective of this book reflects a 'collaborative constructivist' view of teaching and learning. It is recognition of the inseparable relationship between personal meaning making and the social influence in shaping the educational transaction (Garrison and Archer 2000). This unified process recognizes the interplay between individual meaning and socially redeeming knowledge. The recognition of these two interests is crucial in constructing a theoretical framework through which we can understand and apply e-learning for educational purposes.

The intimate relationship between the private and shared worlds is highlighted because e-learning has been most often used to provide more efficient delivery of information and, thus, favour independent learning. The nature of this dominant application is a serious limiting condition to the full utilization of the capabilities of e-learning. While autonomy and access to information are not inherently disadvantageous, there is little recognition of either the transactional nature of an educational experience or of e-learning to support collaborative asynchronous learning. It is the technical capability of e-learning's unique ability to bring together a community of learners, unrestricted by time or place, that must be understood. From this perspective, e-learning would appear to offer the means of creating an educational experience so long idealized in educational theory.

Philosophically, this collaborative constructivist (i.e., transactional) perspective is associated with the work of John Dewey. Dewey rejected all dualistic thinking – particularly with regard to the individual and society. For Dewey, society and the individual cannot exist separately, nor can one be subordinated to the other (Dewey and Childs 1981). To understand education is to understand this interplay between personal interests and experience and societal values, norms and knowledge. This interplay is manifest in the transaction between teacher and student.

Dewey (1938) identified two principles that are reflected in the theoretical framework developed here. One is 'interaction,' which unifies the subjective (personal) and objective (social) worlds in an immediate timeframe. Through this interaction, ideas are generated that illuminate the external world. That is, meaning is constructed and shared. Through interaction, ideas are communicated and knowledge is constructed and confirmed. The second principle is 'continuity,' which goes to the importance of creating the foundation for future learning. As Dewey stated, 'the result of the educative process is capacity for further education' (1916: 68), which has great value for both the individual and society.

Dewey would have embraced the choice and diversity of e-learning with its opportunity for 'active inquiry' and the 'individual variations' it provides; however, he would have also been adamant that discipline required to elevate the process to 'reflective inquiry' be brought to bear on the information. E-learning, and the Internet, are wonderful sources of ideas, but to be 'genuinely educative' they must provide an experience that assures 'continuity' or the foundation for new, worthwhile learning experiences.

The philosophical perspective incorporated in the assumption of collaborative constructivism defines the educational transaction. More specifically, collaboration and constructivism correspond to teaching and learning responsibilities in an educational experience. The teaching and learning transaction is a coherent representation and translation of the dynamics of a collaborative and constructive educational experience.

A transactional view

While knowledge is a social artefact, in an educational context, it is the individual learner who must grasp its meaning or offer an improved understanding. The purposeful process of facilitating an outcome that is both socially and personally worthwhile goes to the heart of the teaching and learning transaction. This transaction is common to all educational experiences, including e-learning.

Thus, an educational experience has a dual purpose. The first is to construct meaning (reconstruction of experience) from a personal perspective. The second is to refine and confirm this understanding collaboratively within a community of learners. At first glance, this dual purpose would seem to reflect, respectively, the distinct perspectives of the teacher and student. However, closer consideration of the transaction reveals the inseparability of the teaching and learning roles and the importance of viewing the educational process as a unified transaction. We are simply viewing the same process from two different perspectives. These two perspectives raise fundamental questions concerning issues of responsibility for learning and control of the process.

Responsibility and control

In an educational transaction, issues of responsibility and control apply to both teaching and learning. The responsibilities of the teacher are complex in that they create and shape the evolving learning environment. This challenge becomes more daunting when powerful technologies are introduced. Teachers must create the cognitive and social conditions that will allow and encourage students to approach learning in a meaningful way. Of course, this demands content expertise, but it is what the teacher does pedagogically that determines the degree to which students assume responsibility for their learning. Having the learner accept responsibility for one's learning is a crucial step in realizing successful educational outcomes – both in terms of specific knowledge structures and in terms of developing the higher-order cognitive abilities that are necessary for continuous learning.

Issues of control apply to both teaching and learning. Education is fundamentally an interactive or transactional process. The challenges and confusion surrounding control issues go to the normative role and responsibility afforded the teacher. It is the teacher who has the legitimate responsibility to define the curriculum and design the educational activities. Unfortunately, there is little opportunity for collaboration in the planning process. That is, the student has little input or influence in planning the process or expected outcomes of the educational experience. This creates the contradictory situation where the student is expected to assume responsibility for activities and an outcome over which they have little input.

The solution inherent to the transactional perspective is to give students opportunities for dialogue regarding outcome expectations, learning activities, and means of assessment. While some aspects of the educational transaction may not be open for negotiation, it is important that students share in this understanding. By being included in the larger process, and being provided choice where appropriate, students are given a sense of control and, therefore, take responsibility for the quality of the educational outcome. Is not the ultimate challenge of the educator to bring students to assume responsibility for their own learning?

The transactional perspective on teaching and learning reflects a dynamic balance of responsibility and control issues congruent with the educational purpose and the capabilities of the students. E-learning draws attention to fundamental responsibility and control issues. Much work is required before we can fully understand the implications that this technology will have on educational transactions.

Theoretical concepts

The key to understanding educational practices is to work back from the desired learning outcomes. In higher education, these outcomes are invariably associated with higher-order learning – becoming a critical and creative thinker. More recently, dispositions such as self-directedness have been added, because it is not a simple matter of having students take responsibility for their learning.

The impermanence of public knowledge, along with the personal challenge of accommodating new ideas and knowledge, necessitates an ability to think critically and be self-directed in managing and monitoring learning. Critical reflection and discourse are also demanded of the teacher for purposes of selecting and organizing content and for diagnosing possible misconceptions and ensuring quality learning outcomes. Critical thinking is a holistic activity incorporating both reflective and shared activities. Critical thinking and discourse is central to the e-learning theoretical framework and is discussed fully in Chapter 6, 'Cognitive presence.'

Critical thinking is a cognitive model that naturally starts from the inside and looks out. This model reflects the various phases of critical thinking that iterate between the private and shared worlds of the individual. The phases of critical thinking (practical inquiry) are the triggering event, exploration, integration and resolution. On the other hand, self-directed learning is a complementary social model that takes an outside perspective and looks in. Self-directed learning addresses issues of management, monitoring and motivation. Self-directed learning is emerging as an important conceptual model towards understanding issues raised by technology that has the potential to transfer enormous control to the learner.

The central role of self-directed learning is concerned with learning management responsibilities and strategies. It is the management of learning, both technically and cognitively, that is fundamentally changing higher education. Technical management speaks to the organization of and access to information, while the cognitive management of learning focuses on the cognitive and metacognitive monitoring of tasks and intellectual demands (e.g., critical thinking). Current practices in higher education restrict the development of management practices, such as self-directed learning, and restrict the use of technologies, such as e-learning, as technical management supports. The role of the learner and modes of cognition are changing by necessity. If e-learning is to be more than simply enhancing current infor-mation-assimilation practices, then both cognitive and technical management strategies must be incorporated.

The concepts of critical thinking and self-directed learning provide the theoretical mechanism for designing and implementing meaningful and worthwhile educational practice. That is, they describe the processes by which effective learning occurs. The next conceptual level in describing effective learning is to address approaches and principles.

Principles

The most promising research and knowledge base for understanding the educational experience has studied the conditions that would facilitate deep levels of understanding, not simply the recall of factual information. This work was pioneered by Marton (Marton and Saljo 1976) and confirmed by Entwistle (Entwistle and Ramsden 1983) among others (Biggs 1987). In its simplest form, this research described two distinct levels of information processing or understanding: surface-level processing, where the student has a reproductive or rote conception of learning and a corresponding learning strategy; and deep-level processing, where the intention is to comprehend and order the significance of the information as well as integrate it with existing knowledge.

It is clear that these approaches to learning and intentions are greatly influenced by the educational environment. That is, students adapt to the expectations and characteristics of the context under the immediate influence of the educator. The mechanism is that context strongly influences students' perceptions of learning tasks and, therefore, the strategies they adopt in approaching learning (Ramsden 1988). This is a rational adaptation to contextual demands on the part of the student in order to ensure a successful outcome. Ramsden (1988) argues that there are three domains that influence perception and subsequent approaches to learning: assessment, curriculum, and teaching. There is, of course, considerable overlap among all three.

Assessment (i.e., testing and grading) has a subtle but pervasive influence in shaping intentions and how students approach an educational experience. In fact, it may well be the most 'critical situational influence on learning strategies' (Ramsden 1988: 164). How they are being assessed sends a very strong signal as to what is important to students and how they should approach learning. If the examination system is information recall, then students will, rationally, prepare for 'recall of factual information to the detriment of a deeper level of understanding' (Marton and Saljo 1976: 125). Obviously, the overwhelming concern of the vast majority of students is to pass. This in turn shapes how students approach learning and, thus, what they will learn. Therefore, assessment must be congruent with intended, desired learning outcomes.

The second domain is associated with curriculum – in particular, workload, or the quantity of material to be assimilated in a defined period of time. Regardless of the student's inherent preference or intelligence, excessive curriculum demands dictate a surface approach to learning. It is not hard to see the influence and negative impact on deep approaches to learning of excessive content expectations beyond the control of the student. An important condition congruent with a deep approach to learning is 'greater freedom to choose content' (Ramsden 1988: 167). The challenge facing students and teachers is that 'the world of knowledge is overwhelming, a vast ocean, horizonless, plunging to impossible depths' (Achenbach 1999: A23). While pedagogy is essential in resolving this challenge, e-learning is an essential tool in creating an environment congruent with deep and meaningful approaches to learning.

Teaching, the third domain, directly addresses this challenge by significantly influencing the approach to learning. The teacher has the greatest influence on shaping the learning environment and learning outcomes. To a large extent teachers define goals, content, and assessment. With the proliferation of information and the convenience of access to this vast ocean of information, it is the primary responsibility of the teacher to chart a way through this chaos, provide order and create the conditions to encourage a deep approach to learning. From the student's perspective, this requires higher-order cognitive processing that includes critical thinking and self-direction.

The transactional perspective for effective teaching means moving beyond simple presentation to facilitative methods (Garrison and Archer 2000). The presentational approach to teaching is highly prescriptive and is exemplified by the large lecture or industrial approach to distance education. The presentational approach is inherently a one-way transmission of information, regardless of efforts to involve the audience. Effective presentation depends on organization, clarity, and enthusiasm. While these are worthwhile teaching characteristics, they have not been shown to be sufficient in and of themselves to encourage or support deep approaches to learning.

As suggested in the phrase itself, the missing element in a presentation approach is interaction or the critical discourse that is central to the transactional perspective. In contrast, the facilitation approach to teaching is based on the ideal of a community of learners and the congruence of discourse with intended outcomes. Effective facilitation may include presentation characteristics, but these must be balanced with flexibility, a supportive climate, and critical discourse. The transactional nature of the facilitation approach allows student participation in setting goals and in selecting content. This demands considerable professional judgment, especially with the freedom and autonomy provided by e-learning.

Teaching principles

Coping with this complexity and the adoption of new technologies necessitates that teachers have a set of guiding principles. Previously, we identified the elements in this quest for quality learning outcomes to include assessment, workload and choice. The following principles reflect a transactional perspective and deep approach to learning. In essence, these principles are intended to create a supportive critical community of inquiry that is core to the e-learning framework described here.

1 Negotiable expectations, clearly expressed, encourage deep approaches to learning.
2 Coherent knowledge structures (schema) facilitate purposeful and integrative learning.
3 Control creates commitment and encourages personal responsibility to monitor and manage meaningful approaches to learning.
4 Choice in content and process is a catalyst for spontaneous and creative learning experiences and outcomes while recognizing and valuing intuition and insight.
5 Critical discourse confirms understanding and diagnoses misconceptions.
6 Critical thinking must be modelled and rewarded.
7 Assessment must be congruent with expected learning outcomes.
8 Learning is confirmed through assessment.

Success in creating an educational community of inquiry requires preparation, sustained presence and considerable pedagogic and content expertise. As we shall see, nothing less than this kind of teaching presence will ensure the full participation of students and deep approaches to learning, regardless whether communication is face-to-face or mediated. In an e-learning context, particular technical characteristics must be understood that directly and indirectly influence approaches to learning.

Teaching and technology

Considering that this book is about understanding the application of e-learning in higher education, we cannot conclude this foundational chapter without considering the contextual influence that technology has had on learning. Knowledge development in this age is a 'technologically aided activity' (Privateer 1999: 62). It is imperative that those involved in higher education come to grips with the reality that technology is an increasingly important element of the educational environment and represents opportunities and constraints for interaction that can significantly influence students' perceptions. With a powerful technology such as e-learning, its influence becomes more apparent, and it becomes more important that we consider that influence. The medium of communication does send a message to the student – and that message can enhance or diminish the intended educational message.

Recently, researchers have come to question statements such as that of Clark, who declared, 'media are mere vehicles that deliver instruction, but do not influence student achievement any more than the truck that delivers our groceries causes changes in our nutrition' (1983: 445). His argument is that it is the instructional design, mediated through learning activities that affect learning outcomes (Clark 1983, 1994).

While the importance of instructional design cannot be denied, the issue is whether this generalization holds across various intended learning outcomes or, to express it another way, whether characteristics of the technology of communication (e.g., e-learning) can, in fact, have a significant influence on higher-order learning (Kozma 1994). That is, is it reasonable to accept the null hypothesis, as stated by Clark and others, that the means of communication have no effect on facilitating critical thinking and discourse or on achieving higher-order learning outcomes?

The research into media use in educational contexts has rather consistently demonstrated no significant differences in learning outcomes when different delivery media were compared (measurements of learning outcomes were based on student examination results) (Russell 1999). However, it is important to note that much of this research did not control for the nature and quality of learning outcomes. In fact, most often the intended learning outcomes measured in these studies were the outcomes expected from low-level, information-assimilation educational experiences, that is, the re-statement of rote-learned facts and static information. But does the 'no significant difference' generalization also hold when higher-order learning outcomes are intended, and where there is a shift in the mode of communication, from oral to written language?

At least one pioneer in the use of written communication for educational purposes suggests that the null hypothesis does not hold. Feenberg states that writing is 'not a poor substitute for physical presence and speech, but another fundamental medium of expression with its own properties and powers' (1999: 345). This echoes comments made by media researchers such as Olson (1994), who asserts that the written language is not just a pale shadow of the spoken language, but rather an independent entity with distinctive characteristics worthy of study in themselves. As Stein (1992) notes, a new, interdisciplinary 'science of the text' is emerging. The issue of text versus speech was also raised as being of particular importance with regard to higher-order learning in Fabro and Garrison (1998).

The differences in the nature of spoken and written communication are, in fact, a key to understanding the effective use of computer-mediated communication and specifically e-learning. The issue of text-based communication is explored more fully in Chapter 3.

The critical point is that contextual variables do influence the nature and quality of learning outcomes. Contextual contingencies and learning activities must be congruent with intended and desired outcomes. What is learned is inseparable from how it is learned (Marton 1988). This, of course, is a crucial realization when utilizing a technology, such as e-learning, that has unique communication characteristics. The method of transmission or communication is an important contextual influence. Educators must be cognizant of the context they are creating from both a pedagogic and technology perspective.

CONCLUSION

The information age and a networked world are forcing educators to rethink the educational experience. It has become very clear that the value-add in a 'knowledge-based future' will be a learning environment that develops and encourages the ability to think and learn both independently and collaboratively. That is, critical and self-directed learners with the motivation and ability to be both reflective and collaborative and, ultimately, with the motivation to continue to learn throughout their lives. Expectations for higher education are rising, and the foundational elements required to realize these higher-order learning outcomes and develop continuous learners have been outlined. This does not represent a reinvention of the educational transaction and learning outcomes. But it does call for a refocusing and rededication to traditional higher-education ideals. These ideals can be brought back within our grasp by technological developments.

Educators are particularly challenged when technologies such as e-learning are inserted into the equation. The reality is that 'digital technologies [e-learning] require radically new and different notions of pedagogy' (Privateer 1999: 70). In this regard, e-learning has considerable potential to alter the nature of the teaching and learning transaction. In fact, it has caused us to face up to some of the current deficiencies of higher education, such as large lectures, while providing possible solutions or ways to mitigate these shortcomings. Seen as part of a pedagogical solution, e-learning becomes an opportunity to examine and live up to the ideals of the educational transaction described previously. Whether we realize the full benefit of e-learning will depend on understanding the context in which it will be introduced.

E-learning is a disruptive technology that is currently influencing how learning is approached in higher education. The question is whether this will be a weak or a strong influence (Garrison and Anderson 2000). That is, will e-learning simply enhance and reinforce existing practices of efficient information dissemination, or will it fundamentally alter how students approach learning and outcome expectations? Higher education will inevitably be forced to recognize the revolutionary nature of learning tech- nologies, and e-learning will be at the forefront. The strong influence of technology will change our ideas and approaches to cognition and pedagogy. As Privateer states: 'It makes little sense for academia to continue a tradition of learning significantly at odds with technologies that are currently altering how humans learn and interact with each other in new learning communities' (1999: 77).

It is the new learning communities and the potential influence of e-learning to which we must turn our attention. The challenge is to understand the emerging educational context and how we create learning environments that will facilitate development of higher-order cognitive abilities and encourage these to thrive in what has been described as the knowledge era. The transactional perspective of teaching and learning adopted here is embedded in a critical community of learners (i.e., community of inquiry) where both reflection and discourse are utilized to facilitate the construction of personally meaningful and socially valid knowledge. It is to this community of inquiry that we turn our attention in the next chapter.

Chapter 3

Community of inquiry

Creating a shared understanding is simply a different task than exchanging information. It's the difference between being deeply involved in a conversation and lecturing to a group. The words are different, the tone is different, the attitude is different, and the tools are different.

(Schrage 1989: 5)

Realizing the potential of e-learning does not imply that traditional educational values and practices will be declared obsolete. In fact, because of e-learning's unique capabilities to support asynchronous, collaborative communication in a dynamic and adaptable educational context, we will see a resurgence of traditional educational ideals, and we will see learners adopting the values of personal responsibility and shared control as their own. However, the educational community has barely begun to appreciate the collaborative capabilities of e-learning and, as a result, these capabilities are greatly under-utilized.

A critical, collaborative learning community has been the *sine qua non* of higher education. Re-valuing the traditional ideal of a community of learners is at the heart of the e-learning transformation. The framework we describe here is based upon the premise (supported by research and experience) that a community of learners is an essential, core element of an educational experience when higher-order learning is the desired learning outcome. By higher-order learning, we mean higher-order thinking 'that is conceptually rich, coherently organized, and persistently exploratory (Lipman 1991: 19). These descriptions are congruent with the often-expressed ideals of higher education that will lead to meaningful, worthwhile, and continuous learning.

The demands of an evolving knowledge society create expectations for individuals to be independent thinkers and, at the same time, interdependent, collaborative learners. These are the very core values and conditions of an educational experience. The creation of knowledge in an educational context is a personally reflective and collaborative process made possible by a community of learners. The idealized view of education, as a critical community of learners, is no longer just an ideal, but has become a practical necessity in the realization of relevant, meaningful, and continuous learning. It is within such a community of learners that the potential of e-learning will be fully realized.

The technology of e-learning has both the capability to precipitate private reflection as well as public discourse within a community of learners. Its power is in its capability to connect people in personal and public ways. This unprecedented capability is fundamentally changing cognitive and pedagogical approaches to teaching and learning. However, along with this technological capability is needed the wisdom to create purposeful yet creative learning experiences with the appropriate balance between reflection and discourse. This balance is found through the teaching and learning transaction within the ethos of an open and critical community of inquiry.

THE LEARNING COMMUNITY

From both theoretical and empirical perspectives, the desirability and effectiveness of collaboration in achieving higher-order learning outcomes is seldom questioned. An increasingly prevalent and accepted position, made more practicable by e-learning, is that 'the teaching of high-level concepts inevitably involves a considerable amount of discourse' (Bereiter 1992: 352). Research in face-to-face and mediated educational contexts confirms the benefits of collaborative learning in supporting higher-order learning (Cecez-Kecmanovic and Webb 2000; Garrison and Archer 2000). While e-learning technologies, unrestrained by time and space 'expand and transform the social interaction space of collaborative learning . . . a deeper understanding of the "inside" of the collaborative learning processes is still missing' (Cecez-Kecmanovic and Webb 2000: 73). If we are to understand how e-learning can change the conditions of the educational transaction, and yet enhance traditional educational values, then we must turn our attention to the understanding of the 'critical community of learners.'

A critical community of learners, from an educational perspective, is composed of teachers and students transacting with the specific purposes of facilitating, constructing, and validating understanding, and of developing capabilities that will lead to further learning. Such a community encourages cognitive independence and social interdependence simultaneously. It is the juxtaposition of both aspects of this seemingly contradictory relationship that creates the spark that ignites a true educational experience that has personal value and socially redeeming outcomes. In many respects, education is a purposeful and guided activity in which the individual is making sense of social experiences. The learning community is a fusion of individual (subjective) and shared (objective) worlds.

E-learning, from an educational perspective, must be appreciated in terms of the nature of the transaction between and among teacher and students. It is a serious mistake to categorize teaching and learning in terms of extreme positions. E-learning is no more inherently learner-centred than traditional face-to-face learning is inherently teacher-centred. Like any educational experience, successful e-learning depends on the ability of the educator to create learning environments that motivate students and facilitate meaningful and worthwhile learning activities and outcomes. The teacher who designs the right balance and blend of collaborative and individual learning activities is the key ingredient.

However, before describing the conceptual framework for a community of inquiry, we first turn our attention to computer-mediated communication and two associated areas of study, which are core to an appreciation of e-learning: computer conferencing and text-based communication.

Computer conferencing

The collaborative potential of Computer Mediated Communications (CMC) for learning was realized utilizing computer conferencing technologies. It was first pioneered in distance education contexts and represented a new era of distance education. This was the post-industrial age, distinguished by its asynchronous, written forms of communication but collaborative approach to distance education (Garrison 1997a). Computer conferencing invariably integrates applications such as e-mail, listserves, and access to information data bases, as well as off-line, computer-assisted learning; however, what really attracted attention to this technology was its ability to support a truly collaborative learning experience, at a distance and independent of time and space. This seriously challenged the dominant world-view of distance education as being a largely independent, self-instructional approach to learning based on mass produced learning packages.

Early in its development, it became apparent that computer conferencing was not an exact replication of the conventional face-to-face classroom experience. As a result, largely of the asynchronous and text-based nature of this communication, many investigators realized that computer conferencing represented a qualitatively different approach to learning (Harasim 1987; Kaye 1987). The unique communication characteristics of CMC have a significant impact on facilitating critical thinking and realizing higher-order learning outcomes. The asynchronous, written nature of most of computer conferencing will be explored briefly in the next section.

The affordability and ubiquity of e-learning, not to mention its capability to support a community of learners, is clearly disrupting the dominant technology in higher education – the lecture. It is fear and uncertainty, a consequence of the lack of a clear model of technologically mediated learning (i.e., e-learning) consistent with the values and ideals of higher education, that limits the wider adoption of computer conferencing and e-learning. Garrison and Anderson (1999) describe an approach consistent with the mandate, culture, and practice of higher education. At the core of this approach is a critical community of learners (teachers and students).

The challenge is to use computer conferencing and its larger complex, e-learning, in ways that support new and more effective approaches to learning. Communications technologies, such as computer conferencing and e-learning 'will reveal new approaches to the teaching and learning trans-action that can enhance the quality of learning outcomes in higher education by increasing access to critical communities of learners, not simply access to information' (Garrison and Anderson 1999: 51). While higher education is not exempt from accessibility demands, we must be clear as to what students should be accessing. Perhaps the best place to start thinking about e-learning is computer conferencing and its ability to support high levels of interactivity, albeit asynchronous. E-learning, properly designed, has all the potential to not compromise the values of higher education, but to create the idealized community of inquiry.

The primary mode of communication in computer conferencing and e-learning is text-based. While educators rely heavily on text-based materials for the transmission of subject matter, oral dialogue dominates the interaction among teachers and students. The fundamental difference is that computer conferencing represents a text-based medium of communication, and this must be understood if it is to be used effectively for educational purposes. To set the stage for understanding communication in a computer-mediated, e-learning context, we will briefly discuss the characteristics of text-based communication.

Text-based communication

It is only in recent decades that linguists, and members of other disciplines dealing with language, regarded speech as clearly the primary form of human language. Writing was seen as the direct transfer of the information conveyed by speech into a different, visible medium. This equivalency assumption is beginning to be considered more closely, particularly within the substantial and rapidly growing body of literature on the use of text-based, computer-mediated communication for educational purposes (Feenberg 1999; Garrison 1997a; Garrison, Anderson, and Archer 2000; Peters 2000).

We argue that the differences in nature between spoken and written communication are, in fact, a key to understanding the effective use of computer-mediated communication and, specifically, the use of computer conferencing in a critical community of inquiry (Archer, Garrison, and Anderson 1999). While e-learning is a powerful communications tool, serious questions have been raised concerning the extent and degree to which text-based communication alters the 'flow and structure' of higher-order teaching and learning, as compared to the more familiar environment of speech-based communication.

A full discussion of the characteristics of text-based communication will not be attempted here. However, we note that there is sufficient evidence to suggest that writing has some inherent and demonstrable advantages over speech when engaged in critical discourse and reflection. One obvious advantage is the permanent record afforded teachers and researchers. This, of course, contrasts with the ephemeral nature of discussions in face-to-face classroom environments. Furthermore, face-to-face conversation is generally less systematic, more exploratory, and less attentive to others' views.

Writing has long been used as both a process and product of rigorous critical thinking. The written word serves best to mediate recall and reflection, while the spoken word functions most effectively to mediate action – usually in face-to-face contexts (Wells 1999). Ong argues that speech is a context which all humans are born into, and that speech is critical to the development of individual consciousness. However, 'writing intensifies the sense of self and fosters more conscious interaction between persons' (Ong 1982: 179). The characteristics of written, as compared to spoken, language would appear to affect the value of the former in facilitating higher-order learning through text-based media such as computer conferencing.

The apparent advantage of the written word in higher-order learning is supported in a study of questioning and cognitive functioning. It was found 'that interaction in this on-line context was more intellectually demanding than that found in face-to-face' (Blanchette 2001: 48). That is, the questions and responses were at a higher cognitive level than in a face-to-face verbal context. A possible (and probable) explanation is the asynchronous nature of written communication. It would appear that, because students have more time to reflect, to be more explicit and to order content and issues, teachers were able to ask higher-level written cognitive questions. Finally, in an on-line context, administrative questions and issues were separated from cognitive questions and discussion. That is, students could focus and reflect on higher-order cognitive questions and their response.

In short, we believe that text-based communication has special attributes to facilitate critical discourse and reflection. There is every reason to believe that text-based communication in an e-learning context would have advantages to support collaborative, constructivist approaches to learning. However, to better understand the nature of text-based communication for educational purposes, we must explore more deeply the environment of a community of learners.

A CONCEPTUAL FRAMEWORK

We have previously alluded to the importance of context and specifically argued for the creation of a community of learners to facilitate critical discourse and reflection. Individual knowledge construction is very much shaped by the social environment. That is, an environment with choice and a diversity of perspectives will encourage critical and creative inquiry. Such a community of inquiry is a requisite for higher-order learning and the core element in the e-learning conceptual framework described here.

Lipman argues for the necessity of a community of inquiry for the operationalization of critical thinking and as an educational methodology. This is a teacher-guided, non-authoritarian community where societal knowledge is revealed in an equivocal, multidisciplinary manner whose goal is to structure relationships (order) to achieve understanding and develop 'rationality tempered by judgement' (Lipman 1991: 8, 14). The community is crucial in precipitating and maintaining personal critical inquiry and the construction of meaning. With the collaboration of the group, the individual assumes responsibility for making sense of the educational experience.

In a community of inquiry there is both rationality and freedom. As Lipman states, a community of inquiry is where

> students listen to one another with respect, build on one another's ideas, challenge one another to supply reasons for otherwise unsupported opinions, assist each other in drawing inferences from what has been said, and seek to identify one another's assumptions. A community of inquiry attempts to follow the inquiry where it leads rather than being penned in by the boundary lines of existing disciplines.
>
> (Lipman 1991: 15)

In other words, a community of inquiry provides the environment in which students can take responsibility and control of their learning through negotiating meaning, diagnosing misconceptions, and challenging accepted beliefs – essential ingredients for deep and meaningful learning outcomes (Ramsden 1988).

There is reason to believe that this inquiry process could be supported in an e-learning context. In fact, considering the reflective and explicit nature of the communication, as well as the opportunity to access unlimited data sources, there is every reason to suspect that there may be distinct advantages to creating a community of inquiry in an e-learning environment.

We have identified in various forms, although not explicitly, the three key elements of a community of inquiry that must be considered when planning and delivering an e-learning experience. They are cognitive presence, social presence, and teaching presence. A brief outline of each is given here. Their implications for ensuring a quality e-learning educational experience are fully

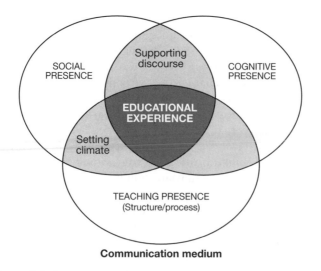

Figure 3.1 Community of inquiry

explored in later chapters. Figure 3.1 shows the relationship of the three elements.

Cognitive presence

At its core, education is about learning, but a specific kind of learning defined by process and outcome. To this end, cognitive presence speaks to intent and actual learning outcomes. We see cognitive presence 'as the extent to which learners are able to construct and confirm meaning through sustained reflection and discourse in a critical community of inquiry' (Garrison, Anderson, and Archer 2001: 11). In essence, cognitive presence is a condition of higher-order thinking and learning.

Cognitive presence is described in the context of a general model of critical thinking. The primary source for this model is Garrison and Archer (2000), but largely derivative of Dewey's (1933) work on reflective thinking. The practical inquiry model, discussed in Chapter 6, is the starting point for understanding and operationalizing cognitive presence. This model represents a generic structure of critical thinking that is consistent with the multiphased educational process designed to construct meaning and confirm understanding.

Social presence

We define social presence as 'the ability of participants in a community of inquiry to project themselves socially and emotionally, as 'real' people (i.e., their full personality), through the medium of communication being used' (Garrison, Anderson, and Archer 2000: 94). When the medium is the written word, establishing social presence can be problematic.

Due to the lack of non-verbal communication, the shift from spoken communication to the written communication of an e-learning context presents a special challenge for establishing social presence. Written communication lacks a sense of 'immediacy' defined as 'those communication behaviours that enhance closeness to and nonverbal interaction with another' (Mehrabian 1969: 203). Immediacy is important to a supportive and secure learning environment because it reduces personal risk and increases acceptance, particularly during critical discourse with its sometimes aggressive questioning and challenging.

Cognitive presence, defined largely as a process of critical thinking, is intimately connected to the learning context. Not only is teaching higher-order cognitive skills more successful when co-operatively based (Resnick 1987), but cognitive presence is enhanced and sustained when social presence is established (Fabro and Garrison 1998; Gunawardena 1995). Socio-emotional communication in text-based communication is possible through the use of compensating strategies, such as the adaptation of textual behaviours to reveal social and relational messages (Walther 1992). Compensating redundancies benefit all communication that carry potential for misunderstanding. Attention must be given to establishing and sustaining appropriate social presence if the full potential of e-learning is to be realized.

Teaching presence

The third mutually reinforcing element in a community of inquiry is teacher presence. One of the difficulties with early computer conferencing was sustaining participation and high levels of discourse (Gunawardena 1991; Hiltz and Turoff 1993). Low levels of interest and participation were rooted in a lack of structure and focus resulting from an excessively 'democratic' approach. While there must be full and open participation, for a purposeful educational experience there is an inherent need for an architect and facilitator to design, direct, and inform the transaction.

Teaching presence is defined as 'the design, facilitation and direction of cognitive and social processes for the purpose of realizing personally meaningful and educationally worthwhile learning outcomes' (Anderson *et al.* 2001). As can be deduced from this definition, teaching presence brings all the elements of a community of inquiry together in a balanced and functional relationship congruent with the intended outcomes and the needs and capabilities of the learners. This, of course, is an enormously imposing task under the best of circumstances. It represents a new, and perhaps greater, challenge in an e-learning context.

The asynchronous nature of e-learning allows opportunities to both engage and disengage. While teaching presence is important to structure learning activities, time discussions, and balance quality and quantity of postings, the teacher must also be a facilitator who models critical discourse and reflection by constructively critiquing contributions (Fabro and Garrison 1998). Unfortunately, much of the e-learning pedagogical guidance to this point is intuitive and sketchy. Much of the second part of this book is devoted to providing practical guidelines based on the community of inquiry framework.

Indicators

For theoretical and practical value, we have constructed a template consisting of categories of indicators within each of the three core elements that reflect meaningful learning activities essential in an e-learning environment. Indicators are key words or phrases that suggest the presence of the three elements and, in total, a quality educational experience. Table 3.1 provides the template that guides our assessment of the nature and quality of an e-learning experience. Ultimately, it will form an analytical tool for educators to assess written transcripts and thereby gauge specifically what is occurring within an e-learning community of inquiry. This template could be an efficient and effective tool when used to suggest the areas of teaching that need to be addressed to optimize the discourse.

The categories for cognitive, social, and teaching presence emerged from the literature and were refined within the community of inquiry conceptual framework. The cognitive-presence categories correspond to each of the practical inquiry phases. Social presence is structured according to affective, open communication and group cohesion. Considerable thought and discussion, based on an exploratory study of computer conferencing

Table 3.1 Community of inquiry categories and indicators

Elements	Categories	Indicators (examples only)
Cognitive presence	Triggering event Exploration Integration Resolution	Sense of puzzlement Information exchange Connecting ideas Apply new ideas
Social presence	Affective Open communication Group cohesion	Expressing emotions Risk-free expression Encouraging collaboration
Teaching presence	Design and organization Facilitating discourse Direct instruction	Setting curriculum and methods Sharing personal meaning Focusing discussion

transcripts, resulted in the three, first-order categories. A similar methodology resulted in the emergence of three teaching-presence categories: design and organization, building understanding, and direct instruction. Examples of indicators for all the categories and elements were initially theoretically derived. However, their validity has been tested and the results are discussed in subsequent chapters.

CONCLUSION

This chapter has outlined the concepts and elements that we believe will provide the order and insight into understanding the complexities and potential of an e-learning experience. Within the conceptual framework of a learning community, we developed the community of inquiry model. The primary elements of a community of inquiry, cognitive, social and teaching presence, were described. Finally, categories and indicators for each of the elements were identified.

The framework and its constituent parts have guided the theoretical and empirical investigation described in this book. We believe it is perhaps the most coherent framework to guide the research and practice of e-learning to this point and that it has enormous potential to structure, guide, and assess e-learning approaches, strategies, and techniques. However, a comprehensive appreciation of e-learning is deficient without grounding in the technological realities and possibilities of e-learning.

Chapter 4

The technology of e-learning

We shape our tools, and thereafter our tools shape us.

(McLuhan 1995: ix)

The Internet and on-line learning currently capture public attention and define today's popular perceptions of educational technology. Yet, it is self-evident that the history of technology in education extends back to the clay tablets, slate drawing boards, and handmade paper of pre-Gutenburgh education. Because of this apparent continuum, some educators like to think of the technologies as being mere tools that are defined and studied as a subset of the way they are used – the instructional design. Others take an opposite approach, defining the educational transaction by the way it is delivered and mediated by a particular technology. This later interpretation echoes Marshall McLuhan's famous dictum that 'the medium is the message' (1995) and seeks to identify the unique technical and cultural features and related symbol sets of each particular medium.

Such attempts at defining education, either totally within or totally outside of the tools used to support, deliver, confine and define it, are each only partial and often misrepresentations of the complex context of any formal education transaction. In this chapter we recognize that the educational technology that sustains the transaction is but one critical component of the educational context. Technology directly affects the display, the interaction, the cost, and the design of the educational outcomes. But it remains only one of many other factors that include both manifest and latent, or hidden, characteristics of the educational context. Other notable components include the instructional design, the effect of evaluation and accreditation, the personalities, motivations, the teaching and learning styles of participants, and the hidden curricula embedded in all formal education contexts.

In this chapter, we will first define educational technologies, then briefly overview their increasing application in education generally and in distance education in particular. We will then discuss the technologies in relation to the creation of three components of formal education: teaching presence, social presence, and cognitive presence. Finally, we will overview the 'hidden curriculum' of educational technologies.

DEFINING EDUCATIONAL TECHNOLOGY

The most common definition of educational technology is based on the 1994 definition by the Association for Educational Communications and Technology (AECT), a professional organization, with perhaps a self-serving motivation, that defines educational technology in extremely broad terms. They first use the term instructional technology, which seems somewhat out of alignment with more recent trends to conceive of and discuss education as both an instructional and a learning event. Nonetheless, they define Instructional Technology as 'the theory and practice of design, development, utilization, management, and evaluation of processes and resources for learning' (Seels and Richey 1994: 129). This definition is far too inclusive to be of practical use, since, for instance, a group of teachers meeting to discuss curriculum reform (development of educational resources) or parents meeting to discuss a behavioural problem in a school (management of process of learning), could each be conceived as engaging in 'instructional technology' applications. Obviously a much narrower definition is needed if it is to aide our understanding of educational technology in e-learning. We need a definition that focuses more on the actual technology and its application in educational settings. However, we recognize the impossibility of discussing or analysing a tool outside of the ways in which that tool is applied and, thus, appreciate that instructional technology implies a discussion of the way in which a tool is used as well as the characteristics, limitations, and applications of that tool.

The word technology drives from the Greek *tekhnologiā*, meaning a systematic treatment of an art or craft (American Heritage Dictionary 2000). This original emphasis on systematic treatment and an implied adherence to tenants of science and especially the scientific method, has inspired the formal field of educational technology to embrace a modernistic, scientific, view of its activities. Kenneth Myers (1999) extends this argument, differentiating between formal instruction and that type of spontaneous and undefined learning associated with information retrieval and display by arguing that 'instruction is not simply a subset of information or a simple interaction with electronic media. Instruction is a design practice with an empirical research background and proven principles and objectives.' This conception of instruction reflects a very strong professional and scientific bias. However, we are not convinced that any profession owns or defines learning – neither in formal educational contexts nor informally in normal life interactions. We are more sympathetic to constructivist notions of education that focus on learner and teacher reflections, appropriations of knowledge, and negotiation of learning objectives.

Our definition of educational technology takes a more popular conception of technology with a focus on tools as opposed to techniques. It may make theoretical sense to think of a lesson plan as a technology, but it confuses both ourselves and the general public when we label all systematic designs, thoughts, expressions, and plans as technologies. Thus, we take a more exclusive definition in this text, defining educational technologies as: 'those tools used in formal educational practice to disseminate, illustrate, communicate, or immerse learners and teachers in activities purposively designed to induce learning.' By focusing on the tools in our definition, we are not implying that study of their multiple and diverse applications is not important. On the contrary, it is this mindful application in a real educational context that we find most intriguing and the motivation for our interest and research.

It has also been popular to consider distance education, and thus e-learning, as a complex system (Moore and Kearsley 1996) composed of institutional, individual, technical, and social components. Such a systems view predisposes us to consider the impact of a change in any one of the component pieces on the complete system. This ecological view is both healthy and necessary as it more accurately describes the e-learning experience as an integrated whole and forces us to look at all related components when making changes in any single subsystem of the whole.

GENERATIONS OF DISTANCE EDUCATION TECHNOLOGY

A major task of scholars and researchers in distance education, as in other disciplines, is to create conceptual models and taxonomies that allow us to better understand the world we inhabit and create. It has been popular to classify the technologies of distance education into so-called generations' (Garrison 1985; Nipper 1989) based largely on the technological tools that support each generation. Both Garrison and Nipper have pointed out, however, that such a strictly technological deterministic point of view is itself biased and they remind us that it is not just the tool, but the way the tool is used and the system that defines the input and outputs to the tool use, that more accurately describes distance education systems. These and other authors have argued that these 'generational' classification systems help us to understand and describe the various components of a system at a given point in chronological space. However, we caution that any discussion that labels particular systems as first generation, as opposed to later generations, carries with it a connotation of linear progress and supplantation of each previous generation by subsequent ones. Such linear 'progress' has not happened. There are still many examples of first- and second-generation distance education systems and technologies serving thousands of learners across the globe. With this in mind, we try to augment a technological view with the pedagogical, administrative, and other systems components associated with each generation in our review of the generations discussion. This approach will help us to place in context the technologies of e-learning.

First generation

The first generation of distance education is marked by features of an industrial model (Peters 1988, 2000) or Fordist (Campion and Williams 1992) organization in which economy of scale is achieved by a Taylorist division of labour, rigid managerial controls, and related methods of accountability. This mass production model allowed distance education systems to create courses and programmes of high quality that could be delivered cost effectively to many thousands of students. A major economic feature of these systems was an increase in the upfront production costs (from those associated with classroom teaching) and a concurrent reduction of variable costs as measured by the cost per student. The technology most associated with this generation is the printed textbook and accompanying course guide. It should not be assumed that these print course materials are merely text or reference books that are typically found in academic libraries. Rather, the material is carefully designed and produced by a purposively selected course team made up of specialized, skilled professionals. Typically the course team in a first-generation system would include:

- an instructional designer familiar with behaviourist learning theory;
- subject matter experts (ideally, but not always, with considerable teaching experience acquired in both campus and face-to-face contexts);
- graphic artists capable of illustrating complex events and creating a consistent and graphically stimulating look and feel to the materials;
- editors capable of translating all team production in language that is appropriate to the targeted learning group; and
- a project manager to manage budgets and time lines and to facilitate collaboration and coordination of various course components.

The tone of all the materials, and especially the course guide, is crafted to reflect a conversational approach between the absent instructor and the independent student. Thus, it conveys a sense of 'guided didactic interaction' (Holmberg 1989) that is designed to create a vicarious relationship between the course team members (primarily the subject matter experts) and the individual students.

The pedagogy of first-generation systems is based on behaviourist notions of accountability, observability, and the division of complex concepts into easily understandable subcomponents. The teacher's task in B. F. Skinner's words is 'the arrangement of contingencies of reinforcement under which students learn' (Skinner 1968: 64). What students learn is very explicitly defined and is based on positivistic notions that there is a common reality and from it objective learning objectives can be extracted. Great emphasis is placed on the creation and subsequent testing of learning objectives so that knowledge acquired is manifest and can easily be discerned and demonstrated by students for accreditation purposes.

A defining feature of first-generation technology is the maximization of freedom and independence for students. Students no longer have to wait until a specific time of the year to commence studies, nor are they compelled to work to an institutionally defined timeline derived from the expected norm of effort and time commitment of a cohort of students. Individual students may complete learning activities and challenge tests and examinations at a speed they alone define. First-generation distance education systems have been labelled independent study – implying that students work independently and not as members of a group. Defenders of these systems have been quick to point out, however, that students studying under such systems are not independent learners in the sense that they are isolated from the guidance of a teacher. Originally, such interaction was sustained in asynchronous format through mail, but in modern first-generation systems, e-mail and telephone are more commonly used.

First-generation systems can very easily be translated to the Web and are often used in e-learning contexts. However, simply substituting screens for paper and the Internet for postal delivery does not produce effective e-learning content. First, there are questions of formatting, colour and other graphic details that require changing as the display media changes. Second, adherence to pedagogical models based on independent study, preclude peer interaction and collaborative learning. Third, the behaviourist notions of simplicity and content disaggregation do not mesh well with the fragmented display and organization of information found in real life and especially in networked contexts. Finally, standalone, first-generation text does not take advantage of the hyperlinking capability of the Web, nor of access to the vast array of information and knowledge resources available for exploration and discovery on the Web. However, first-generation study guides are almost always one component of a quality e-learning environment.

Second generation

The second generation evolved within an era defined by the newer technologies of mass, broadcast media and a growing acceptance of cognitive learning theory. This generation retained an emphasis on independent study in that there were seldom restrictions on time or place of study (beyond access to the ubiquitous radio and television). Large and, often, expensive media productions (telecourses) were created that allowed students to virtually visit the laboratory, the workplace, or to stay within the classroom with the audio and/or video images of their teachers. Advances in cognitive learning theory led to the use of advanced organizers, role models, summary reflections and simulated peers to draw the user into a sophisticated media world. However, direct interaction between students and teachers was restricted to the technologies associated most often with the first generation – telephone and mail. In the second generation, course teams got much larger as full production crews added skill, perspective, and a great deal of cost to the materials. Such high, front-end costs drove the need for large student populations to amortize costs and the attempt (only sporadically successful) to market second-generation courses to a global market. Bates (1995) notes that second-generation technology supported more interaction between students and delivery institutions. However, the 'teacher' was often not the creator of the course content but rather a course tutor whose task was to support and evaluate student achievement. A recent addition to second-generation distance education is the attempt to deliver 'interactive, computer-assisted instruction courses' to students using networked or independent computers (i.e., PLATO system) with courseware conveyed on CD-ROM or DVD disks. To date, these attempts have been less than successful.

The use of enhanced second-generation tools such as computer-assisted instruction through use of simulations, multimedia drill and practice, and self-paced tutorials has flourished on the Net. These programs, often written to execute on students' machines (as opposed to a central server) can provide very effective additions to e-learning programming. However, the cost of such enhancements is high, and the skills required to produce these 'educational objects' are usually beyond those of typical teachers. These cost and distribution problems gave rise to the development of centralized and distributed libraries of educational objects, such as MERLOT (http://www. Merlot.org), which are increasingly useful tools for finding, accessing, and assessing e-learning course content.

Third generation

The third generation takes advantage of the capacity for both asynchronous and synchronous human interaction provided by a variety of telecommunications technologies – notably audio, video, and computer mediated conferencing. Some authors (Taylor 2001) have argued for a differentiation between the interactive capacity of video and audio teleconferencing and the computer enhanced (and usually asynchronous) nature of computer-mediated communications, thereby creating a fourth generation. However, as we have noted, the Net continues to expand its capacity to deliver all modes of human communication in both asynchronous and synchronous modes, thus making such a distinction too narrow to designate as a new generation. The third-generation distance-education system embraced constructivist learning theories to create opportunities for students to create and re-create knowledge, both as individuals and as members of learning groups. This knowledge construction takes place within the negotiation of content, assignments, and projects and is elaborated on in the discussion, collaborative projects, and resource- or problem-based curriculum designs that define quality, third-generation programming.

Fourth generation

A number of authors (Lauzon and Moore 1989; Taylor 2000) have suggested that a fourth generation has emerged that combines the first three major attributes of the Net: information retrieval of vast amounts of content; the interactive capacity of computer mediated communications (CMC); and the processing power of locally distributed processing via computer-assisted programming, usually written in Java. Obviously, these are powerful new tools, but their substantiation in new models of distance education programming, beyond the capability of integrating CMC and Web resources (via development and delivery packages such as WebCT, Blackboard, Lotus Notes, etc.) is as yet quite rudimentary.

Despite the lack of full adoption of features ascribed to fourth generation by most distance-education programming, Taylor (2001) has articulated a fifth generation that he describes as the 'intelligent, flexible learning model.' To the earlier generation of Web-based resource access and synchronous and asynchronous communications, Taylor adds key 'intelligent functions' – namely the use of automated responses to frequently asked questions and an integration and related access via 'portals' to campus-based resources and services. He describes the development of a fifth-generation system at the University of Southern Queensland's e-University Project. We don't find the current application of 'intelligence' as exemplified in Taylor's examples compelling reason to define a new generation. Perhaps of greater interest in Taylor's fifth generation is the integration of other components of the distance education system into the delivery system for instructional content. Through the use of Web-based administration, student records, library, and other administrative and student support services, this fifth generation represents an integrated system of administrative, support, and instructional components. Given the ubiquitous access to each component of these critical systems through a common set of Web-based tools, the fifth generation promises to add significantly to the institutional and service capacities for those institutions capable of marshalling the necessary administrative and technological expertise and the funding to achieve this high level of integration.

Besides administrative advantage we also expect rapid development of pedagogical innovations in the fifth generation. The use of teacher and student agents that incorporate various types of intelligence and that will allow fruitful searching, navigation, and exploitation of the 'semantic web' should occur. The fifth generation, to summarize, adds artificial intelligence to the Web or, as the original designer of the Web, Berners-Lee describes it, builds semantic meaning into the Web, such that it can be navigated and processed by both humans and nonhuman 'autonomous agents' (Berners-Lee, Hendler, and Lassila 2001).

This review of so-called 'generations of distance education' reveals that the type, extent, and integration of various types and modes of interaction is the defining component of each generation. Kaufman (1989) noted linear progression between generations of educational technology in terms of quantity and quality of interaction between students and teachers in subsequent generations and further noted increases in student power to influence content and an increased emphasis on thinking skills as opposed to demonstration of comprehension. Further, we see that the technology of the Web seems to have an increasing role in each generation, such that it is perhaps the only technology associated with fourth- and fifth-generation distance-education systems. We thus digress slightly to look at the Net in terms of a universal interaction service in distance education.

THE NET AND DISTANCE EDUCATION

A major problem for authors attempting to describe the impact of the Internet on distance education is the ethereal nature of the Web itself. The Net is constantly evolving and changing as applications are developed that exploit its capacity for information communication and processing. Resnick (1996) captured this sense well when he noted that:

> The Internet acts as a type of Rorschach test for educational philosophy. When some people look at the Internet, they see it as a new way to deliver instruction. When other people look at it, they see a huge database for students to explore. When I look at the Internet, I see a new medium for construction, a new opportunity for students to discuss, share, and collaborate on constructions.

The impact of the Net on media used in distance education is illustrated in a diagram we developed in 1990 (Figure 4.1). It illustrates the various educational technologies used in distance education. The diagram roughly situates each of the technologies on the vertical access by the degree of interaction supported by the technology and on the horizontal access by the degree of freedom of time and distance allowed to participants in the interaction.

A refinement of the diagram a decade later (Figure 4.2) shows the comprehensive power of the Net to subsume almost all of the discrete capabilities of the earlier technologies. Further, the cost of interaction and

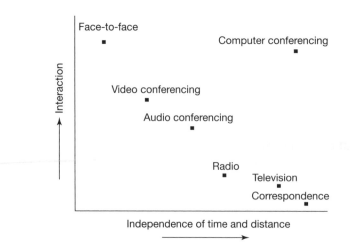

Figure 4.1 Distance education media

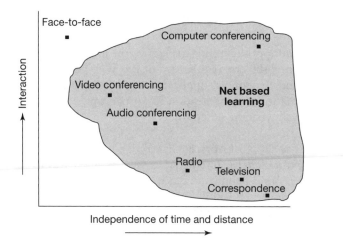

Figure 4.2 Educational media

information dissemination by the Net is, in many cases, a fraction of the cost associated with production and distribution via the earlier discrete technologies.

Despite the impressive convergence and cost cutting associated with the Web for educational delivery, we are convinced that the Net's real potential for education is still some years from realization. The original conception and construction – the WWW – was an information storage and retrieval device (Berners-Lee 1999). The systematic storage, retrieval and re-use of information has always been a defining feature of formal education, as illustrated by the location of the world's first universities in conjunction with collections of rare texts in monastery libraries. The capacity to deliver, monitor and retrieve results of educational computer programming (simulations, drill and practice, tutorials, etc.) has allowed a re-emergence of interest in computer-assisted instruction and the development of immersive environments (Dede 1996) as tools for distance education. But, the emergence of the Net as a medium of communication adds the most critical feature of the formal education process – interaction between and among teacher, students, and content. We now turn to a more detailed discussion of the various forms of interaction that define distance-education programming.

EDUCATIONAL TECHNOLOGY AND INTERACTION

Interaction (in many formats) has been a defining feature of formal education. John Dewey's 'transactional' concept of an activity-based education describes an education experience as a 'transaction taking place between an individual and what, at the time, constitutes his environment . . .' (1938: 43). Dewey's description fits neatly with the complex shifting of time and place that defines e-learning and further emphasizes the importance of interaction with the various human and non-human actors that constitute the environment. For Dewey, interaction is the defining component of the educational process and occurs when students transform the inert information passed to them from another and construct it into knowledge with personal application and value (Dewey 1916).

This stress on interaction is reinforced by Laurillard who argues that a university education must go far beyond access to information or content and include 'engagement with others in the gradual development of their personal understanding' (2000: 137). This engagement is developed through interaction between teachers and students and among students, and forms the basis of her conversational approach to teaching and learning. Garrison and Shale (1990) define all forms of education (including distance education) as interactions among teachers, students, and content. Thus, both human and non-human interactions are integral and reciprocal components of a quality e-learning experience.

Both classroom teachers and researchers have stressed the value of interaction within the educational process. For example, Palloff and Pratt argue that 'key to the learning process are the interactions among students themselves, the interactions between faculty and students, and the collaboration in learning that results from these interactions' (1999: 5).

Michael Hannafin (1989) itemizes the five functions that technologically mediated interaction purports to support in an educational context. These functions are:

1 Pacing: Interactive pacing of the educational experience operates from both a social perspective and serves to keep an educational group synchronized or acting together, and in an individual perspective, serving to define a speed for progressing through the lesson such that the educational objectives are completed in a reasonable and pedagogically effective span of time. Allowing individual student control of pacing and at the same time facilitating group pacing such that collaborative learning activities are possible, is a challenge to interactive forms of e-learning and one that requires careful balance and planning during the instructional design.

2 Elaboration: Interaction serves to develop connections between new content and existing mental schema allowing learners to build more complex, memorable and transferable connections between existing and new information and skills. In the process of explaining their conceptions to others, the explanations grow and are cross linked with schemas built around internal course constructs and those built in the career and personal experience of students.

3 Confirmation: This most behavioural function of interaction serves both to reinforce and shape the acquisition of new skills through selective reinforcement. Confirmational interaction traditionally takes place between student and teacher. However, it is also provided by feedback from the environment through experience and interaction with content in laboratories, through programmed computer response in interactive tutorials, simulations and games, and from peers in collaborative and problem based learning.

4 Navigation: This function prescribes and guides the way in which learners interact with each other and content. Adequate navigation becomes especially critical when students are confronted with the mind numbing quantity and variety of paths available on the Web.

5 Inquiry: Hannafin's concept of inquiry in 1984 focused on inquiry to the computer system that was displaying content and monitoring student response. The interconnected and greatly more accessible context for inquiry now provided by the Internet opens the door to a much greater quantity and quality of inquiry. However, the interactive capability for students to follow individual interests and paths makes inquiry both a motivating and personalizing function of interaction.

To these we add a sixth, 'the study pleasure and motivation' that Holmberg (1989: 43) describes as developing from interaction and relationships between the teaching and learning parties. This motivation not only leads to socially induced pleasure for many students but also induces the critical attention to detail and involvement that Langer (1997) defines as 'awareness' and ascribes as the most important determiner of learning.

It can be seen that interaction fulfils many critical functions in the educational process. However, it is also becoming more apparent that there are many types of interaction and indeed many actors (both human and inanimate) involved.

The Web as a communications tool has been developed and refined to simulate all of the formats undertaken using earlier technologies – including the face-to-face classroom. To illustrate the multiple ways in which the Net supports educational interaction we present a diagram of the six interactive dyads possible among the three critical actors in a formal educational context – students, teachers, and content. See Figure 4.3.

E-learning technologies have developed to the extent that quality teacher–student activities can be supported either among groups or individually, and in either real time (synchronously) or in delayed time (asynchronously). Below, we briefly review the six forms of interaction supported via e-learning (Anderson and Garrison 1997).

Teacher–student interaction

Much has been written about the appropriate interaction between students and instructors (Dewey 1933; Laurillard 1997). Although much of this research has been grounded in study of classroom behaviour, our own work, and that of others, has extended study of teaching, cognitive, and social presence in an e-learning context. This research suggests that many of the qualities of interaction in e-learning contexts can be both defined and measured and have impact on learning outcomes. (See, for example, Garrison, Anderson, and Archer 2000; Rourke and Anderson 2002; Rourke *et al.* 1999, 2001.)

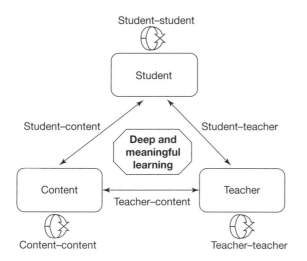

Figure 4.3 Modes of interaction

Student–student interaction

Collaborative and co-operative learning was not available to students involved in earlier generations of distance education (i.e., correspondence). Work on the social construction of knowledge (Rogoff 1990), situated learning (Lave 1988), and social cognition (Resnick 1991) and the application of these theories to education have resulted in a rich and growing body of knowledge. Most of this research has focused on classroom-based delivery, largely with school-age children. However, adult, and especially professional, learners have also been shown to benefit from interaction with others with common professional concerns (Brookfield 1987; Schön 1988). In an e-learning context this interaction is supported through a variety of communications technologies, in both synchronous and asynchronous formats.

A problem with many forms of student to student interaction theory is that they nearly always assume that individuals share a content interest within a shared time space. However, it is also known that some students actively choose distance education formats – including e-learning – that allow for study that is independent of intense contact and the temporal restraints associated with paced and interactive forms of education delivery. E-learning expands the rich tradition of independent study associated with earlier generations of distance education and provides and often mandates a variety of synchronous and asynchronous learning activities. The design of appropriate amounts of interaction is critical and depends on a variety of factors, many of which are rooted in the expectations and capacity for interaction expressed by the students. We can no longer assume that distance education is either an individual or a collaborative process.

Student–content interaction

The majority of student time in all forms of education is consumed by interactions with educational content. In traditional, classroom-based education, this has meant study using texts and library resources. In e-learning contexts, content can be expressed in text for reading on screen or on paper, but content is often supplemented with a rich variety of computer assisted instruction, simulations, micro worlds, and presentation creation tools. In particular, work with the development, cataloguing, and distribution of such content, broadly referred to as 'learning objects', promises to provide teachers, developers, and students with a vastly expanded set of content (Downes 2000).

In the past, content was assumed to be static and inert – waiting for consumption by students. Now content can be animated and given agent-like properties of autonomy, volition, and rationality and can be programmed to take a more active part in student–content interactions. The development of learning heuristics that allow for adaptation by content in response to student performance and request allows for an individualized form of student–content interaction.

Teacher–content interaction

The first of three forms of interaction initially highlighted by Anderson and Garrison (1997) is interaction between teachers and content. The development and application of content objects has become an increasingly important component of the teacher's role in both distance and classroom-based education. The semantic network provides opportunities for teachers to find, utilize, and, in some cases, create learning objects that are automatically updated by other content agents, by emerging data, and by other research results or environmental sensors. For example, content objects can be created that display and then calculate trends from real-time data sources such as economic indicators, news broadcasts, temperature, and other sensory data. Content agents can also be built that will monitor and report on research activities of researching teachers, thus creating new content automatically that both informs and involves students in the research process.

Teacher–teacher interaction

The pervasive existence of low-cost, multimedia networks is providing unprecedented opportunities for teacher–teacher interaction. Security concerns and the high cost of travel is propelling the search for ways in which distributed teachers can engage in quality teacher–teacher interaction while keeping physical travel to minimal levels. In 1992 we organized the first virtual conference ever held on the public Internet (Anderson and Mason 1993). Since then, a variety of increasingly sophisticated networking tools have been built to support both synchronous and asynchronous forms of teacher–teacher interaction. Recent interest in peer-to-peer technologies that support document sharing, text and audio conferencing, and calendar coordination (http://www.groove.com) herald a new era of sophisticated support for teacher–teacher interaction that is not dependent on centralized network servers. It is crucial that these types of networking tools be exploited if e-learning teachers are to take maximum advantage of developments in their own disciplines and of developments in e-learning pedagogy. This interaction between and amongst teachers forms the basis of a learning organization within the educational institution. Anderson, Varnhagen, and Campbell (1998) found that the first and most important source of assistance and insight into both technical and pedagogical challenges comes from colleagues close at hand to the individual teacher.

Teacher–teacher interaction is the cornerstone of community within which teachers function. This community has been recognized by constructivists (Coleman, Perry, and Schwen 1997; Wenger 2001) as essential in providing the multiple perspectives needed to develop instruction in complicated domains and especially multicultural domains common to e-learning.

Content–content interaction

Computer scientists and educators are creating 'intelligent' programs or agents, that 'differ from conventional software in that they are long-lived, semi-autonomous, proactive, and adaptive' (MIT 2000). Agents are currently being developed and deployed that are capable of retrieving information, operating other programs, making decisions, and monitoring other resources on the network. We can imagine an era when content is automated to update itself from various sensory inputs and then to alert students and teachers when these alterations reach a noteworthy level. The most common example of agents are Internet search engines, or spiders, that are continuously scouring the networks and sending the results of their discoveries back to central data bases. In the not-too-distant future, teachers will create and use learning resources that continually improve themselves through their interaction with other intelligent agents.

THE SEMANTIC NETWORK AND E-LEARNING

It is difficult to overestimate the impact of the Net on most aspects of twenty-first-century society and its institutions. Though we don't go quite so far as Oracle Corporation's advertising slogan that 'The Internet changes everything', we do believe that the emerging global network has already had profound effects on the formal education process, and promises to contribute even more as the technologies mature and our capacity to manipulate them effectively increases. Further, we believe that the development, over the next decade, of the 'semantic web' (Berners-Lee, Hendler, and Lassila 2001) promises to create an intelligent network, designed for use by both humans and mobile agents, that will simultaneously lead to rapid enhancements of the communication, retrieval, and information processing capacities of the Net.

Higher education, like many other businesses, is being challenged to find ways to operate more effectively and efficiently. As with other post-industrial enterprises there is pressure to realize these economies by substituting the high cost associated with human labour for that of machines. This 'commodification' has been decried by neo-Luddite critics of higher education (Noble 2002; Winner 1997), but they have provided little data to show that such substitution reduces learning, or even decreases satisfaction of faculty or students. This pressure for economy leads to ongoing discovery of ways in which student interactions with teachers can be substituted by lower cost interaction with other students and with interactions with content. Such substitution is not easy as there are many unique factors in student–teacher interaction most especially dealing with affect, power spontaneity and immediacy which create significant challenges for educators seeking to reduce the costly time commitments of student–teacher interaction.

There are, however, two technological factors propelling efforts to meet the challenges of creating quality student–content and student–student interactions. The first is the ongoing power and sophistication of machines and their capacity to act autonomously and with varying degrees of judgment, which we may call machine intelligence. This development is illustrated by Moore's Law, which states that the number of transistors on a chip (significant components of processing power and speed) doubles every 18 months. Thus, computer scientists and educators have machines that are twice as powerful as their predecessors every 18 months. The second technological driver is encapsulated in Metcalf's Law, which states that the power of a network is proportional to the square of the number of nodes in that network. Thus, increasing the size of a network increases its functionality and usefulness geometrically. These two technological drivers, increasing processing power and functionality of networks, give rise to significant increase in the capacity of content to interact more effectively and efficiently with human interactors. For example, the I Help system, designed at the University of Saskatchewan (Vassileva *et al.* 1999), allows each student to create an agent that negotiates with other agents to facilitate one-to-one tutoring and response to individual questions by available students at any time located anywhere on the Internet. We expect more such agent tools to evolve in the next decade, bringing the benefit of mediated interaction to students and teachers anywhere and at any time.

CONCLUSION

In this chapter we have overviewed the various technologies used to create the context of e-learning. We examined the technologies in terms of progressive generations and we conclude that all five generations exist simultaneously on the Web today. E-learning takes components of each generation, digitizes them and delivers them using a common interface (the Web browser) and common transportation protocol (TCP/IP). Integral to the technologies utilized in e-learning is the capacity to support interaction. This interaction focuses on that involving students – between and among other students, faculty, and non-human forms of content. However, the interaction between teachers, teachers and content, and among content agents themselves, are growing capacities that aid and enhance e-learning program development and delivery. The future of Web technology focuses on the capacity of the Net to support not only human, but the interation of agents serving humans. We will take a final look at these emerging capacities in Chapter 11.

Chapter 5

Social presence

> the core competency of universities is not transferring knowledge, but developing it, and that's done within intricate and robust networks and communities.
>
> (Brown and Duguid 1996: 13)

The early adopters of e-learning immediately recognized its potential to support a collaborative learning experience. Along with this, however, came the challenge of creating a learning environment that would serve the educational needs for which it was intended. This precipitated considerable thought and discussion with regard to replicating a classroom experience. What was not fully appreciated was that creating a community of learners through an asynchronous text-based means of communication represented a qualitative shift from that of a real-time, verbal, face-to-face mode of communication. As such, the challenge of creating a cohesive community of inquiry in a medium that provides no visual cues other than words or images on a screen presents a unique challenge for educators.

We need to understand the nature of social interaction in a non-verbal environment and how this can be utilized to create a community of inquiry. A cohesive community can be created based upon establishing friendships or it can be based upon other common purposes such as specific educational goals. A community will sustain itself based upon how well individuals and the group meet their needs and achieve their goals. Each of these purposes will create different climates and be effective in realizing different outcomes. We focus our attention here on creating a community or social presence within an e-learning context.

A NON-VERBAL COMMUNITY

Community is integral to all aspects of life. It is the fusion of the individual and the group; the psychological and sociological; the reflective and the collaborative. This is no less so from a learning or educational perspective. This implicit denial of community has been perhaps the greatest shortcoming of traditional distance education with its focus on prescriptive course packages to be assimilated by the student in isolation. Unfortunately, this is based upon an assumption that learning is an individual experience and that there is little need to negotiate meaning and confirm understanding. Education and learning, in its best sense is a collaboration, which includes a sense of belonging and acceptance in a group with common interests. As such, we must reflect upon what social presence means in an e-learning community distinguished by its predominant mode of communication.

Social presence is defined here as 'the ability of participants in a community of inquiry to project themselves socially and emotionally, as 'real' people (i.e., their full personality), through the medium of communication being used' (Garrison, Anderson, and Archer 2000: 94). It is inconceivable to think that one could create a community without some degree of social presence. However, social presence becomes more specific and demanding when the community is one of inquiry. Inquiry involves sustained critical discourse (i.e., cognitive presence). Social presence must be congruent with inquiry and the achievement of specific learning outcomes. So why is this important and what does this look like?

Asynchronous text-based communication would appear to present a special challenge in creating a social environment and community of inquiry. Communication theorists have drawn considerable attention to the lack of non-verbal communication cues that are considered to be crucial in forming collaborative relationships. Short, Williams, and Christie concluded a review of media studies by stating that the 'absence of the visual channel reduces the possibilities for expression of socio-emotional material and decreases the information available about the other's self-image, attitudes, moods, and reactions' (1976: 59). The authors use the term 'social presence' to argue that the medium is a serious limiting factor to a shared social presence. The question is whether this is fatal to forming and sustaining a fully collaborative community of inquiry. Does text-based communication provide the means to communicate socio-emotional content necessary for building a social community, of feeling connected and preventing a feeling of anomie? Can teachers and students acquire and use compensating communication skills for quality collaborative learning experience?

In a visual and verbal context, cues such as body language and verbal intonation can have a profound effect on how a message is interpreted. Can the nature of written language compensate for the lack of these other cues? Does written language provide other means to communicate socio-emotional cues? Or, on the other hand, might this medium provide an advantage to the less extraverted student and, overall, offer the potential for greater equality and participation? The simple answer to these complex questions is that it has been shown that students can and do overcome the lack of non-verbal communication by establishing familiarity through the use of greetings, encouragement, paralinguistic emphasis (e.g., capitals, punctuation, emoticons), and personal vignettes (i.e., self-disclosure) (Rourke and Anderson, in press).

The implicit understanding of the purpose of a community of inquiry carries with it social cues to help shape the nature of the interaction that is appropriate and required. This is more explicitly defined and reinforced through teaching presence. Under these circumstances, the fact that text-based communication is a relatively lean medium may not be a serious limitation. As we have argued, the characteristics of a text-based medium as being reflective, explicit, and precise may well have inherent advantages in focusing and elevating the cognitive level of the exchange. That is, the communication may well be more effective for facilitating critical thinking and discourse. The conclusion here is that the apparent limitations of text-based e-learning may well provide advantages not possible in a face-to-face educational context. The leanness or richness of the medium may well be defined by the task at hand (i.e., purpose) and by the compensating opportunities afforded by the medium. The research conducted on text-based e-learning has consistently demonstrated a capacity for a high level of socio-emotional interpersonal communication (Rourke *et al.* 1999).

We argue that social presence is an important antecedent to collaboration and critical discourse. Establishing relationships and a sense of belonging are important. However, on the other hand social presence does not mean supporting a 'pathological politeness' where students will not be sceptical or critical of ideas expressed for fear that they might hurt somebody's feelings and damage a relationship. Social presence means creating a climate that supports and encourages probing questions, scepticism and the contribution of more explanatory ideas. This is where e-learning with appropriate teaching presence can be a very effective medium for supporting an intellectually challenging yet respectful, and a personal yet focused community of inquiry. It is through balancing these seemingly contradictory elements that a quality learning environment is created.

CATEGORIES OF SOCIAL PRESENCE

The classification scheme for social presence was constructed through an iterative process. This consisted of a theoretical analysis of the literature as well as the analysis and coding of computer conferencing transcripts. This resulted in three broad categories of social presence indicators consisting of affective, open communication, and cohesive communicative responses (see Table 5.1). Sharing socio-emotional feelings is innate to the communicative functionality and cohesion of a community of inquiry.

Table 5.1 Social presence classification and indicators

Category	Indicators	Definition	Example
Affective	Expression of emotions	Conventional expressions of emotion, or unconventional expressions of emotion, includes repetitious punctuation, conspicuous capitalization, emoticons	'I just can't stand it when . . . !!!!' 'ANYBODY OUT THERE!'
	Use of humour	Teasing, cajoling, irony, understatements, sarcasm	The banana crop in Calgary is looking good this year ;-)
	Self-disclosure	Presents details of life outside of class, or expresses vulnerability	'Where I work, this is what we do . . .' I just don't understand this question'
Open communication	Continuing a thread	Using reply feature of software, rather than starting a new thread	Software dependent, e.g., 'Subject: Re' or 'Branch from'
	Quoting from others' messages	Using software features to quote others' entire message or cutting and pasting selections of others' messages	Software dependent, e.g., 'Martha writes:' or text prefaced by less than symbol <
	Referring explicitly to others' messages	Direct references to contents of others' posts	'In your message, you talked about Moore's distinction between . . .'
	Asking questions	Students ask questions of other students or the moderator	'Anyone else had experience with WEBCT?'
	Complimenting, expressing appreciation	Complimenting others or contents of others' messages	'I really like your interpretation of the reading'
	Expressing agreement	Expressing agreement with others or content of others' messages	'I was thinking the same thing. You really hit the nail on the head'
Cohesive	Vocatives	Addressing or referring to participants by name	'I think John made a good point.' 'John, what do you think?'
	Addresses or refers to the group using inclusive pronouns	Addresses the group as we, us, our, group	'Our textbook refers to . . .', 'I think we veered off track . . .'
	Phatics, salutations	Communication that serves a purely social function; greetings, closures	'Hi all,' 'That's it for now' 'We're having the most beautiful weather here'

Affective responses

Affective responses are not only a defining characteristic of social presence but of participation in a community of inquiry. Interest and persistence is essential to a learning experience and is very much an affective response. These emotions are a facilitating condition for engagement in meaningful dialogue and an educational experience. Respectful and supportive socio-emotional responses reflect the conditions necessary for critical reflection and discourse. Affective responses are a tacit recognition of a reciprocal relationship with the community.

There are three major indicators of an affective communicative response (see Table 5.1). First, when physical cues and vocal intonations are not present, expression of emotions are made possible through other means such as punctuation, capitalization, and emoticons. This is demonstrated clearly in the simple examples provided in Table 5.1. Second, beyond these more unconventional means of expressing feelings, language itself is a very powerful communicator of emotion. Perhaps the easiest to appreciate is related to humour and similar expressions, such as teasing. These expressions convey goodwill and suggest that there are no serious personal challenges. Third, another very human way of establishing an emotional relationship or bond is through self-disclosure. Basically, the more we know about other members of the community, the more trustful and responsive we become.

Open communication

Affective responses have a direct effect on interactivity and open communication. Open communication is reciprocal and respectful, which is core to deep and meaningful learning outcomes. Open communication has an affective quality that reflects a climate of trust and acceptance. It allows questioning while protecting self-esteem and acceptance in the community. Open communication is built through a process of recognizing, complimenting, and responding to the contributions of others, thereby encouraging reflective participation and interaction. Expressing agreement, as well as questioning the substance of messages, reveals engagement in the process of critical reflection and discourse. Open communication is about relevant and constructive responses to the questions and contributions of others. The inherently reflective and insightful communication in an e-learning experience is built entirely upon open communication.

Cohesive responses

All the previous indicators contribute directly to the third category of social presence – group cohesion. Group cohesion is essential to sustain the commitment and purpose of a community of inquiry, particularly in an e-learning group separated by time and space. More specifically, constructing meaning and confirming understanding can only be sustained in a cohesive community. When students perceive themselves as part of a community of inquiry, the discourse, the sharing of meaning, and the quality of learning outcomes will be optimized. The builders of cohesion begin with indicators such as addressing others by name. Group cohesion and association is taken to the next level by using inclusive pronouns such as 'we' and 'our.' Other salutations, such as 'Hi all,' also build and reflect group cohesion.

PRACTICAL IMPLICATIONS

The fundamental question is: how does one establish social presence in an e-learning environment that will support a community of inquiry and the concomitant, critically reflective discourse? The key to answering this question is recognizing that there may be an optimal level of social presence. Too little social presence may not sustain the community. On the other hand, too much social presence may inhibit disagreement and encourage surface comments and social banter. After all, the primary goal is not simply social interaction and sustaining the group for the group's sake. The group sustained by social presence is a means to an end. The end being a quality learning experience for each and every student.

This issue of social presence supporting a larger purpose was brought to our attention by Liam Rourke, our research assistant, during the research on this topic. Reflecting the students, he stated:

> Despite theoretical rumours to the contrary, students do not complain that computer conferencing is asocial, terse, hostile, etc. On the contrary, if students complain, it is that the conference is too social, too polite, not critical or challenging, and thus not a productive learning experience.
>
> (Rourke 2000, personal communication)

From a social-presence perspective, the greatest challenge in an e-learning context is to ensure a cognitively stimulating and productive learning environment. The criticism from students was that there was a 'tone of decency' that translated into 'warm feedback' and students not being challenged. A student summed up this 'pathological politeness' phenomenon (a phase coined by our colleague Walter Archer) in the following manner:

> In the context of the [group], it was important to differentiate trust – a willingness to make oneself vulnerable to colleagues – from congeniality. The first is genuinely the basis for posing challenging questions; the latter can actually stand in the way of 'straight talk.'

This is a crucial distinction for the teacher when creating a community of inquiry and facilitating critical discourse. It is respect, not necessarily being liked.

More specifically, while these indicators have some empirical validity (Rourke *et al.* 1999), they are not all of equal importance in establishing social presence. For example, humour must be used carefully or it can isolate individuals. Due to the risk involved in using humour effectively in a lean, text-based medium, examples of humour are not commonly found in e-learning communities. Certainly, if it is to be used, it is perhaps best to wait until social presence is firmly established and the personalities of the individuals have been revealed sufficiently.

Another important factor in establishing social presence is the example set by the teacher. Modelling of appropriate messages and responses can be crucial in making students feel welcome and in giving them a sense of belonging. These messages and responses should set the tone and draw reluctant participants into the discussion. For this reason, the teacher or moderator must be particularly sensitive and responsive at the start of an e-learning experience. We must keep in mind that the purpose of establishing a secure environment is to facilitate critical thinking and inquiry. In this regard, there is some inherent risk in challenging fellow students', not to mention the teacher's, assertions. This is where the teacher, in encouraging questioning of his or her own comments, can be an excellent model. The tone is set by the teacher in making all participants feel this is acceptable and not a personal attack.

Finally, if possible, consideration needs to be given to an initial face-to-face meeting of the group. This can have an accelerating effect on establishing social presence and can shift the group dynamics much more rapidly towards intellectually productive activities. Learning activities that may be more effectively or efficiently conducted in a face-to-face setting could also be scheduled at this time. Such blended approaches have strong advantages that go beyond social presence. The downside is, of course, the loss of freedom with regard to time and location. This may well be a worthwhile trade-off.

CONCLUSION

The previously described indicators can provide a good idea of the level of social presence in a text-based e-learning community of inquiry. While strong social presence does provide the basis for respectful questioning and critique, it does not guarantee an optimally functioning community of inquiry. There must be an effective presence of the remaining elements of a community of inquiry – cognitive and teaching presence – to establish the optimal level of social presence for the specific educational goal. It is the elements of cognitive and teaching presence that take a community beyond the largely social function to one of inquiry. To understand the transition of a group to the function of inquiry, we turn next to cognitive presence.

Chapter 6

Cognitive presence

> How shall we treat subject matter . . . so that it will rank as material of reflective inquiry, not as ready-made intellectual pablum to be accepted and swallowed just as if it were something bought at a shop.
> (Dewey 1933: 257)

> Knowledge exists . . . only in minds that have comprehended and justified it through thought.
> (Paul 1990: 46)

In an e-learning context, the challenge for participants to communicate their thoughts and insights is no less formidable than creating a social presence. However, while social presence is an essential element of a community of inquiry, the purpose of that community is more than social interaction. The purpose of an educational community of inquiry is invariably associated with intended cognitive outcomes. That is, cognitive processes and outcomes are at the core of the transactions. Social presence and even teaching presence are, in most respects, facilitators of the learning process. That is not to diminish their importance, but to recognize the ultimate purpose of an educational experience. The goal here is to provide an explanation of the nature and quality of discourse conducted in a text-based environment.

It is to the learning experience and the required cognitive presence that we focus our attention. We use the concept, cognitive presence, to describe the intellectual environment that supports sustained critical discourse and higher-order knowledge acquisition and application. More specifically in the context of this discussion, cognitive presence means facilitating the analysis, construction, and confirmation of meaning and understanding within a community of learners through sustained discourse and reflection largely supported by text-based communication.

CONCEPTUAL BACKGROUND

The theoretical framework and context for this discussion have been described previously in Chapters 2 and 3. The foundational framework is the community of inquiry model with the three overlapping elements of social, teaching, and cognitive presence. In this section we turn our attention to the genesis and manifestation of the cognitive presence concept.

Critical thinking

Cognitive presence is closely associated with the concept of critical thinking. The concept of critical thinking utilized here is derived from Dewey's (1933) reflective thinking model. For Dewey, reflective or critical thinking has practical value in that it deepens the meaning of our experiences and is, therefore, a core educational aim. Critical thinking both authenticates existing knowledge and generates new knowledge, which suggest an intimate connection with education. The other dimension that must be noted is the interplay between the private and public worlds. Lipman argues that the objective of the reflective paradigm is 'intellectual autonomy' (1991: 19) but, in reality, is 'thoroughly social and communal' (1991: 14). This raises the notion of a community of inquiry discussed in previous chapters. The importance of this concept for an educational experience is reflected by Lipman when he states that if 'education is to prepare students to live as inquiring members of an inquiring society, then that education must be education as inquiry as well as education *for* inquiry' (1991: 246).

Critical thinking is synonymous with inquiry. However, what we mean by critical thinking is not self-evident. The reason, among others, for selecting Dewey's concept of reflective thinking is that it is comprehensive and coherent. Most forms of thinking (e.g., creative, critical, intuitive) can be interpreted within this framework (Garrison and Archer 2000). Critical thinking is viewed here as an inclusive process of higher-order reflection and discourse. In an attempt to integrate various overlapping concepts associated with reflective and critical thinking, Garrison and Archer (2000) offer a generic model of critical thinking and intuition, with its genesis in Dewey's phases of reflective thought, that considers imagination, deliberation, and action. (See Figure 6.1.)

Perhaps the key element of this model is the overlay of the concept of the public and private worlds on the five phases. This is particularly relevant in an e-learning experience considering its mostly asynchronous and text-based environment. There is, in fact, a remarkable bias towards a balance between reflection and discourse. This is contrary to verbal discourse, which is biased to a spontaneous and less reflective process. This, of course, has its advantages and disadvantages. This recognition of two realities is an advantage in appreciating that while all phases have elements of reflection and discourse

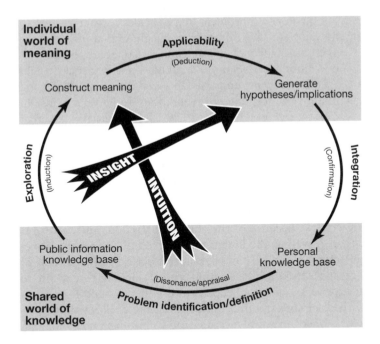

Figure 6.1 Critical thinking and intuition

(unity principle), one phase may emphasize discourse over reflection and vice-versa. Because reflective and discourse activities cannot be separated in practice, this is an educational tool.

This model is useful in making sense of related concepts such as creative thinking, problem solving, intuition, and insight (Garrison and Archer 2000). First, creative thinking is clearly a divergent process focused on the early stages of critical thinking. On the other hand, problem solving is mostly focused on convergent thinking that emphasizes the latter phase of the critical thinking process. That is, the goal is a solution to a relatively narrow problem. The differences between creative thinking and problem solving are a question of emphasis and purpose as both processes include elements of the other and engage all phases of critical thinking.

Second, concepts and processes related to intuition and insight cannot be ignored. These are important aspects of rational thought and are not simply mystical processes to be rejected as unworthy of understanding. While there is an affective dimension to intuition and insight, they are important creative and subconscious inductive processes that are, according to Dewey, a 'product of practical deliberation' (J. Garrison 1997: 33). Intuition is not an 'out of the blue' experience but is preceded by purpose and considerable reflective thinking. Moreover, like insight, it inevitably results from a deep and integrated understanding of a phenomenon. It is generally a vague, inexact awareness of the key to a problem that provides useful direction to clearly explicate the solution. This differs from insight in that insight is the classic 'eureka' experience where clear solutions or coherent conceptualizations occur. While intuition arises more directly from experience, insight arises as a result of reflection (being immersed in a well-defined problem) and the generation of tentative conceptual representations. Intuition and insight is the union of perception and reason (Dewey 1967) and essential to coherent systemic thinking. Perception is explicitly represented in the practical inquiry model discussed subsequently.

Educators seek to understand these cognitive processes in order to allow them to design more natural and less contrived educational experiences that recognize how individuals reconstruct experience and construct meaning and not simply condemn them to assimilating inert knowledge. This is important in an e-learning context because of the cognitive freedom and control it affords the learner as well as the integration of the public (collaborative) and private (reflective) worlds. The collaborative yet reflective process of e-learning has great potential for facilitating critical thinking that is core to an educational experience. The challenge is to use this to build the critical spirit along with discipline-specific, critical-thinking abilities developed through the process of constructing meaning and confirming understanding.

For purposes of simplicity, we define critical thinking in terms of practical inquiry (Garrison and Archer 2000). Cognitive presence is seen to be defined and manifested through the practical inquiry model.

Practical inquiry

Practical inquiry is grounded in experience (Dewey 1933). The integration of the public and private worlds of the learner is a core concept in creating cognitive presence for educational purposes. The two-dimensional, practical-inquiry model is presented in Figure 6. 2. The continuum between *action* and *deliberation* is reflected in the first dimension of the model. The transition between the concrete and abstract worlds is reflected in the *perception–conception* dimension of practical inquiry. This second dimension reflects the cognitive process of associating facts or events and ideas or concepts. As well as being a practical guide to designing and facilitating a cognitively worthwhile e-learning experience, this model has framed our research into e-learning.

The practical inquiry model includes four phases (trigger, exploration, integration, and resolution) in describing cognitive presence in an educational context generally, and in e-learning specifically. These phases are core to describing and understanding cognitive presence. To start, we must reiterate that these phases are not immutable. They are generalized guidelines that, in practice, may be 'telescoped' or reversed as insight and understanding is either

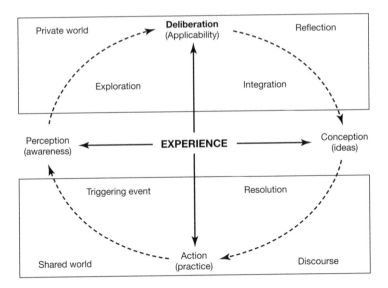

Figure 6.2 Practical inquiry

achieved or blocked. However, a metacognitive understanding of all phases can be of enormous value to both teacher and student in assessing the task at hand and progress achieved – not to mention the ultimate goal of learning to learn.

The first phase of practical inquiry is the initiation or triggering event. In a somewhat contrived educational experience (i.e., teacher defines classroom expectations), this needs to be a well-thought-out activity to ensure full engagement and buy-in from the students. It should also speak to a core organizing concept or issue. Preferably, this would be a dilemma or problem that students could relate to from their experience or previous studies. While the responsibility of the teacher is to initiate this phase of inquiry, this can be structured in a more open manner by framing the issue and eliciting questions or problems that students see or have experienced. This has several positive outcomes in terms of involving students, assessing of the state of knowledge, and generating unintended but constructive ideas.

The second phase of practical inquiry is exploration. This means to first understand the nature of the problem and then to search for relevant information and possible explanations. This may be done through group activities and brainstorming and/or through more private activities such as literature searches. Here students will experience iteration between the reflective and shared worlds as ideas are explored collaboratively and individuals try to make sense of what may seem to be complexity and confusion. This, however, is the essence of a true community of inquiry. The educational challenge is to manage and monitor this phase of divergent thinking in such a way that it begins to be more focused in preparation for the next phase.

The third phase, integration, moves into a more focused and structured phase of constructing meaning. Decisions are made about integration of ideas and how order can be created parsimoniously. While this is a highly reflective phase, students are also intimately engaged in critical discourse that will shape understanding. It may well be during this phase of the inquiry that the characteristics of e-learning come to the fore. The asynchronous and explicit nature of text-based communication may well facilitate deep and meaningful learning outcomes. For these very reasons, this is a particularly challenging phase for creating cognitive presence. In terms of assessing the depth or quality of learning outcomes, the teacher must probe for understanding and misconceptions as well as model the critical thinking process. The tendency is to become entrenched in the exploration phase and not move to more advanced phases of inquiry. Creating cognitive presence necessitates engaging students in all the phases of practical inquiry, including a metacognitive appreciation of the phases and challenges they are experiencing.

The fourth phase is the resolution of the dilemma or problem, whether that be reducing complexity by constructing a meaningful framework or discovering a contextually specific solution. This confirmation, or testing, phase may be accomplished by direct or vicarious action. Direct confirmation is more difficult and often impractical in an educational context. However, in an e-learning environment, with students operating out of work or family contexts, direct applications and testing may be more realistic. In any case, vicarious or mental modelling of solutions are viable and worthwhile educational activities. In good educational environments, as in real life, resolution is seldom fully achieved. Inevitably, results of the resolution phase raise further questions and issues, triggering new cycles of inquiry and, thereby, encouraging continuous learning.

COGNITIVE PRESENCE DESCRIPTORS

Practical inquiry is the model within which we assess cognitive presence. The goal is to provide a practical means to judge the nature and quality of critical reflection and discourse in a collaborative community of inquiry. We believe the descriptors and indicators of cognitive presence generated in our research have considerable potential to assess the quality of inquiry. The goal is to use these indicators to assess critical thinking and discourse with regard to the developmental phases of practical inquiry. This much-needed guide accommodates assessment of the nature of critical discourse when dealing with large numbers of messages generated over the course of an extended e-learning experience. After all, the purpose is to facilitate discourse to achieve the greater purpose of achieving higher-order learning outcomes. In this regard, attention to process, in terms of ensuring progression of reflection and discourse through to resolution (i.e., understanding), is essential.

While not currently a reality, the ideal would be an automated tool that practitioners could use to do rough content analyses of e-learning transcripts. This tool would provide teachers with a means of quickly assessing the nature of the discourse (i.e., phase of practical inquiry) and inform them of whether direct intervention is required to move the discussion forward. Even without this automated tool, descriptors and indicators corresponding to the phases of practical inquiry can provide the means to assess cognitive presence through what are lean clues (individual thought processes) embedded in text-based transcripts.

Table 6.1 provides the descriptors (adjective characterizing process) and indicators (manifest examples) that correspond to each phase of the practical inquiry process. These were first based on the socio-cognitive processes that characterized each of the phases of practical inquiry. They were then enhanced and confirmed empirically (Garrison, Anderson, and Archer 2001).

The first phase, the triggering event, is associated with conceptualizing a problem or issue. For this reason we consider this evocative and inductive by nature. The educational processes would include presenting information that generates curiosity and questions. It should also further discussion in a way that builds into subsequent phases of inquiry. An example might be a statement and question such as: 'It has been argued that the only way to deliver effective e-learning is through a community of inquiry model or

Table 6.1 Practical inquiry descriptors and indicators

Phase	Descriptor	Indicator
Triggering event	Evocative (inductive)	Recognize problem Puzzlement
Exploration	Inquisitive (divergent)	Divergence Information exchange Suggestions Brainstorming Intuitive leaps
Integration	Tentative (convergent)	Convergence Synthesis Solutions
Resolution	Committed (deductive)	Apply Test Defend

approach. However, this approach is not well understood or implemented. Why do you think that is?'

The second phase, exploration, is a search for relevant information and ideas. For this reason, this is an inquisitive and divergent process. The educational process would include brainstorming ideas; offering supportive or contradictory ideas and concepts; soliciting narratives of relevant perspectives or experiences; and eliciting comments or responses as to the value of the information or ideas. Following the previous theme, a typical statement corresponding to the exploration phase might be: 'One reason I think it is seldom used is that it is too complicated to get co-operation. Another may be the mind-set of those in charge to change practices.'

The third phase, integration, is the process of constructing a meaningful solution or explanation. Therefore, this is considered to be a tentative connection of ideas capable of providing meaning and offering potential solutions. The educational transaction would include: integrating information; offering messages of agreement; building on other ideas; providing a rationale or justification; and explicitly offering a solution. An example would be: 'We also had trouble getting co-operation. Often the use of new tools requires new organizational structures. We addressed these issues when we implemented a systems approach, and I think that's why we were successful.'

The fourth phase, resolution, critically assesses the viability of the proposed solution through direct or vicarious application. Resolution requires a commitment to test the solution deductively, perhaps through a vicarious implementation or thought experiment. This would require a rigorous analysis of the hypothetical test, which could take the form of a presentation and defence with other participants critiquing the suggested application. On the other hand, the test could take the form of a direct application or action research project – either an individual or group project. An example of an exchange consistent with this phase of practical inquiry might be: 'A good test would be to ensure that participants understand the expectations, and that collaboration is properly rewarded. Once implemented, this could be assessed by considering project grades as well as the impressions of the participants.'

As revealed in our research, the challenge for educators is to move the discussion and individual cognitive development through each of the phases of practical inquiry. That is, to build the discussion from problem recognition (triggering event) through to exploration, integration and resolution. The tendency is to do the first two phases very well, the third phase less well, and the last phase hardly at all (Garrison, Anderson and Archer 2001; Kanuka and Anderson 1998). We speculate that this is very likely due to the democratic nature of the medium and lack of a strong teaching presence. There must be an appreciation of, and commitment to, the value of thinking progressively through a problem and dilemma such that some worthwhile and long-term benefit ensues. This, of course, is the essential purpose of an educational experience.

What is most required to create cognitive presence and higher-order learning outcomes consistent with the intended goals and expectations of the e-learning experience is a moderator who can assess qualitatively the nature of the discourse and then proactively shape it following the critical thinking cycle. Considering the somewhat ethereal nature of e-learning, it is important that participants be encouraged to relate the ideas and concepts to work and family contexts. This will focus the discourse on integration and resolution. Moreover, the likelihood of this progressive development of the cognitive process happening is greatly enhanced with a metacognitive understanding of critical thinking and practical inquiry (i.e., cognitive presence). It may also be extremely helpful to creating cognitive presence for all the participants to also have a metacognitive appreciation of what they are doing and why.

CONCLUSION

The cognitive presence framework provides insight into the cognitive aspects of an e-learning experience and a means to assess the qualitative nature of that discourse. In turn, assessing the nature of the discourse can provide insights into the nature of the teaching and learning transaction and what interventions may be appropriate. While much work remains to refine this tool empirically, the practical inquiry model, with its indicators, is a good heuristic method of guiding and assessing the nature and quality of cognitive presence.

Chapter 7

Teaching presence

> Although you are guided by a clearly defined organizing vision, you change your methods, content, and evaluative criteria as you come to know more about the ways these are perceived by students.
>
> (Brookfield 1990: 30)

Because of the expanded educational opportunities and choices, teaching in an e-learning context is an onerous responsibility. The frame of e-learning extends interaction, choice, and movement, and this has a liberating and transformational effect on approaches to teaching. To not recognize this, to use the restricted frame of traditional classroom presentational approaches, is to ignore the capabilities of the medium and induce conflict. Implicit in this recognition is the need to rethink how we approach teaching in an e-learning context and how we examine the nature of our intended learning outcomes. Despite the unknowns associated with designing and delivering a meaningful and worthwhile e-learning experience, it is clear that these technologies provide enormous choice that cannot be ignored. Moreover, it will be through the presence of a competent and responsible teacher that this potential will be realized.

With the expanded capabilities and choices that e-learning presents, it is natural to shift towards an interactive and inquiry-based approach. This shift, which favours learner control and responsibility, has biased e-learning to a 'guide on the side' approach. We argue that this is a learner-centred approach rather than a learning-centred approach. From a formal learning or educational perspective this distinction is more than a subtlety or nuance. Education is a unified process where teachers and students have important, complementary responsibilities. This relationship is at the heart of an educational experience. The focus is on learning, but not just whatever the learner capriciously decides. An educational experience is intended to focus on learning outcomes that have value for society as well as the learner. A learner-centred approach risks marginalizing the teacher and the essential value of the transaction in creating a critical community of inquiry. In an educational experience, both the learner and teacher are part of the larger process of learning. Teaching presence is charged with shaping the right transactional balance and, along with the learners, managing and monitoring the achievement of worthwhile learning outcomes in a timely manner.

In most cases, simply re-assigning responsibility and control to the learner violates the intent and integrity of the educational experience to facilitate a critical and constructive learning process. Teaching presence performs an essential service in identifying relevant societal knowledge, designing experiences that will facilitate critical discourse and reflection, and diagnosing and assessing learning outcomes. With e-learning, this is both easier and more difficult. It is easier in the sense that the medium supports thoughtful dialogue. It is also more difficult in that this medium is inherently different and requires new approaches. E-learning demands greater attention to balancing control and responsibility, but the result can be very rewarding.

To establish appropriate teaching presence, it is necessary to go beyond suggestions or techniques that lack a true understanding of the medium. This lack of perspective was clearly evident in a recent survey of college faculty who had incorporated on-line or Web-based learning in their teaching. Faculty wanted

> 'more pedagogical tools, advice, and communities for their on-line teaching and learning efforts. . . .' In particular, they asked for tools that would foster greater student critical and creative thinking in their Web-based teaching efforts. Finally, there was a felt need for on-line teaching guidance, mentoring, and expert answers to problems.
>
> (Bonk and Dennen, in press)

Clearly, more effort and creativity must go into understanding and appreciating the integrating element of teaching presence to facilitate critical thinking and higher-order learning outcomes within an e-learning context.

ROLES AND FUNCTIONS

The role of the teacher in e-learning will change – but for the better. In its best sense, the core principles and responsibilities of a traditional educational transaction are translatable to an e-learning context. While effective teaching can take different forms, principles such as clear expectations, critical discourse, and diagnosis of misconceptions are common to both face-to-face and e-learning environments. The responsibilities of teaching in any context are complex and multifaceted. They include being a subject matter expert, an educational designer, a social facilitator, and a teacher. However, as has been noted, the liberating frame of e-learning significantly alters how these responsibilities are fulfilled.

There is remarkable consistency across the literature as to the categories of teaching presence associated with an e-learning context. Although there has been some shifting of roles across the categories, there is a close mapping of the previous classification schemes associated with e-learning and the three categories of teaching presence adopted here. Table 7.1 demonstrates the remarkable consistency of the various teaching roles across each of the contributions. These are reasonably intuitive but also have some empirical support (Rossman 1999; Anderson *et al.* 2001). The intuitiveness and consistency of these elements provide confidence and understanding upon which to further explore and explicate teaching presence in an e-learning context.

Table 7.1 Teaching roles in e-learning

Anderson et al.	Berge	Paulsen	Mason
Instructional design and organization	Managerial	Organizational	Organizational
Facilitating discourse	Social	Social	Social
Direct instruction	Pedagogical Technical	Intellectual	Intellectual

As noted in Table 7.1, the educator's roles fall into three primary categories: design and organization, facilitating discourse, and direct instruction. Consistent with this we define teaching presence as 'the design, facilitation, and direction of cognitive and social processes for the purpose of realizing personally meaningful and educationally worthwhile learning outcomes' (Anderson *et al.* 2001: online). From this description, there should be no doubt of the essential role teaching presence plays in integrating the various elements of an educational experience made ever more challenging by the possibilities of e-learning.

Before describing each of the elements of teaching presence in detail, it should be emphasized that teaching presence is what the teacher does to create a community of inquiry that includes both cognitive and social presence. Therefore, we do not focus specifically on the social and cognitive elements themselves but on the roles of a teacher or the actual functions that a teacher must perform to create and maintain a dynamic learning environment. These functions are integrative in the sense that teaching presence brings together the cognitive and social in purposeful and synergistic ways. It will be noted that there is a cognitive bias in teaching presence and that social presence is in the background. For example, the social element of previous researchers is reframed from the perspective of discourse, which, of course, has a social origin.

Identifying more precisely indicators and corresponding examples for each of the teaching presence categories can provide useful guidelines, especially for those less familiar with e-learning methods. Detailed descriptions of each of the three elements of teaching presence follow.

DESIGN AND ORGANIZATION

Design and organization has to do with macro-level structure and process. Perhaps not surprisingly, the design and organization of an e-learning course of studies is, at least initially, more demanding than the design and organization of a similar course of studies in a traditional classroom context. This is due, first, to the technology and the need for teachers to redesign approaches to teaching and learning to maximize the capabilities of the medium. In some cases, this redesign may be a considerable undertaking. Those who have, in the past, relied exclusively on lecturing will find a much greater need to focus on the design and organizational element of teaching when moving to an e-learning method. This need is further compounded by the fact that many students will not have experienced an e-learning course, and new expectations and behaviours will require understanding and practice.

Building the curriculum is made more complex by having to both increase and decrease content. Increased in the sense of providing links to other sites that may include important learning objects or supplementary material. Decreased in the sense that, if there is to be considerable interactivity, repurposing lecture notes and reducing the quantity of material presented cannot be ignored. In conjunction with this broadening and channelling of course materials is the crucial task of selecting both individual and collaborative activities and estimating the time to be spent on each. It is here that an understanding of the medium intersects with the actual teaching and learning transaction. The design work at the front end of a course of studies will pay considerable dividends during the course and its benefits will be reflected in the results. It will not, however, preclude in-process organizational decisions. Table 7.2 provides the design indicators along with exemplars.

Design and organization provide the macro-level structure for any learning experience and have similar responsibilities and functions. The semantic difference is that design refers to structural decisions made before the process begins, while organization refers to similar decisions that are made to adjust to changes during the learning–teaching transaction (i.e., in situ design). Organizational comments reflect the flexible and non-prescriptive nature of any educational experience. Design is but a flexible template, created with the expectation that specific issues and needs will inevitably arise that will necessitate alterations in the course of action.

Table 7.2 Instructional design and organization indicators

Indicators	Examples
Setting curriculum	'This week we will be discussing . . .'
Designing methods	'I am going to divide you into groups, and you will debate . . .'
Establishing time parameters	'Please post a message by Friday . . .'
Utilizing medium effectively	'Try to address issues that others have raised when you post'
Establishing netiquette	'Keep your messages short'
Making macro-level comments about course content	'This discussion is intended to give you a broad set of tools/skills which you will be able to use in deciding when and how to use different research techniques'

The interactivity of e-learning places an increased importance on organizational issues. The indeterminate nature of the entry and development of knowledge in students will inevitably introduce some uncertainty into the design process. If e-learning is to be a collaborative, constructivist process, then students must have some influence on what is studied and how it is approached. Therefore, design should not be separated from delivery. It continues in the guise of organizational responsibilities, and, as such, there are considerable advantages to ensuring continuity from the design to the organization phase. This is best accomplished when a teacher can both design and organize the educational experience in a way which will introduce effective responsiveness to developing needs and events.

FACILITATING DISCOURSE

The second element of teaching presence, facilitating discourse for the purpose of building understanding, goes to the heart of the e-learning experience. Facilitating discourse recognizes the role of the community of inquiry as enabling and encouraging the construction of personal meaning as well as shaping and confirming mutual understanding. This element represents the fusion of purpose, process, and outcome. It is where interest, engagement, and learning converge.

The teacher plays an essential role in facilitating discourse in an e-learning experience. Managing and monitoring discourse in an e-learning context is no less important than in face-to-face discussions. The reflective and rigorous nature of text-based communication demands serious commitment. To sustain this commitment and encourage quality contributions requires that the discourse be focused and productive. The risks of doing otherwise are reflected in the following words of caution with regard to facilitating an e-learning conference:

> unless the teacher facilitates the networking activities skillfully, serious problems may develop. A conference may turn into a monologue of lecture-type material to which very few responses are made. It may become a disorganized mountain of information that is confusing and overwhelming for the participants. It may even break down socially . . . rather than building a sense of community.
>
> (Harasim *et al.* 1995: 173–174)

The teaching responsibilities here require sustained attention to a broad range of issues. The overriding concern is to establish and sustain the learning community. This demands attention to both cognitive and social presence concerns. Postings must be closely monitored and the nature and timing of responses must be carefully considered. The community must be somewhat self-sustaining; therefore, too little or too much teaching presence may adversely affect the discourse and the process of building understanding. While maintaining this balance, teacher postings must model the critical quality of the discourse and also shape it to constructive learning outcomes. Guidance is also required to engage less responsive students as well as curtail the exuberance of those who tend to dominate the discussion. These skills are not so different from facilitating a face-to-face discussion.

At the same time, the challenge is to not simply encourage or even reward prolific responses. The teacher must demonstrate appropriate and relevant responses, bring attention to well-reasoned responses, and make linkages to other messages. Participants must feel the discussion is moving in a purposeful direction and in a timely manner. At the right time, the threads of the discussion need to be brought together and shared understanding explicitly stated. All of this requires more than a 'guide on the side' but less than a 'sage on the stage.' That is, the teacher must negotiate something more substantial than a rambling conversation but not just a prescriptive dissemination of information. When students take responsibility for collaboratively constructing and confirming understanding, teaching presence has found the appropriate balance of control. Some indicators and examples of facilitating discourse are shown in Table 7.3.

Facilitating discourse for purposes of building understanding involves pedagogical, interpersonal, and organizational issues. Teaching presence must be as concerned with cognitive development as with a positive learning environment, and it must see content, cognition, and context as integral parts of the whole. Some messages are primarily social, occur in chat rooms, and are generally off-limits to the teacher. Others are more complex and embed

Table 7.3 Facilitating discourse indicators

Indicators	Examples
Identifying areas of agreement/ disagreement	'Joe, Mary has provided a compelling counter-example to your hypothesis. Would you care to respond?'
Seeking to reach consensus/ understanding	'I think Joe and Mary are saying essentially the same thing'
Encouraging, acknowledging, or reinforcing student contributions	'Thank you for your insightful comments'
Setting climate for learning	'Don't feel self-conscious about 'thinking out loud' on the forum. This is a place to try out ideas after all'
Drawing in participants, prompting discussion	'Any thoughts on this issue?' 'Anyone care to comment?'
Assessing the efficacy of the process	'I think we're getting a little off track here'

various cognitive and social elements. This is where the full skills of a teacher and facilitator come to bear.

DIRECT INSTRUCTION

Direct instruction goes beyond that of a facilitation role and is most often associated with specific content issues, such as diagnosing misconceptions. The teacher's scholarly leadership manifests itself in this situation and is often quite specific in nature. Although this is a legitimate and important authoritative influence, this essential teaching responsibility has been either ignored or downgraded. Disciplinary expertise and efficient shaping of the learning experience are essential aspects of any educational experience. The risk in e-learning is that the proper educational and intellectual climate may be lost with anomie resulting.

The potential for direct instruction challenges the 'guide on the side' concept. While this concept may have some value at times, in and of itself it is limited as an approach to e-learning. It suggests an artificial separation of facilitator and content expert, and speaks to the potential distortion of an educational experience that has become pathologically focused on student-centredness to the exclusion of the influence of a pedagogical and content expert in the form of a teacher. Such a laissez-faire approach misinterprets the collaborative–constructivist approach to learning and the importance of systematically building learning experiences (i.e., scaffolding) to achieve intended, higher-order learning outcomes.

Table 7.4 Direct instruction indicators

Indicators	Examples
Present content/questions	'Bates says . . . what do you think'
Focus the discussion on specific issues	'I think that's a dead end. I would ask you to consider . . .'
Summarize the discussion	'The original question was . . . Joe said . . . Mary said . . . we concluded that . . . We still haven't addressed . . .'
Confirm understanding through assessment and explanatory feedback	'You're close, but you didn't account for . . . this is important because . . .'
Diagnose misconceptions	'Remember, Bates is speaking from an administrative perspective, so be careful when you say . . .'
Inject knowledge from diverse sources, e.g., textbook, articles, Internet, personal experiences (includes pointers to resources)	'I was at a conference with Bates once, and he said . . . You can find the proceedings from the conference at http://www . . .'
Responding to technical concerns	'If you want to include a hyperlink in your message, you have to . . .'

Teaching presence, as defined here, is not possible without the expertise of an experienced and responsible teacher who can identify the ideas and concepts worthy of study, provide the conceptual order, organize learning activities, guide the discourse and offer additional sources of information, and diagnose misconceptions and interject when required. These are direct and proactive interventions that support an effective and efficient learning experience. Indicators and examples of direct instruction are shown in Table 7.4.

CONCLUSION

The categories of teaching presence provide a template that can be of considerable value to structuring, facilitating, and directing an e-learning experience. Notwithstanding the essential role of a teacher, it needs to be emphasized that in a community of inquiry, which frames all of our discussions, all participants have the opportunity to contribute to teaching presence. In fact, if the ultimate goal is to learn to learn, students must be encouraged to become self-directed and to manage and monitor their own learning appropriate to the task and their ability. This becomes even more obvious when we suggest designating student moderators. For these reasons, we have not referred to this concept as *teacher* presence but rather as *teaching* presence. As participants develop cognitively and socially, the more distributed teaching presence will become.

Up to this point we have provided the framework and elements of an e-learning experience. We have not attempted to identify principles or suggest specific guidelines with regard to the practice of e-learning. The challenge is to suggest activities that capitalize on the characteristics and potential of the medium in use. This means thinking differently about what an e-learning experience can be. It means recognizing the possibility of creating a collaborative, critical community of inquiry that is rich and accessible. This necessitates that we conceive of the role of the teacher not in a diminished but in a different presence. While many of the teaching responsibilities remain, they will most assuredly reveal themselves in a different form. In the next section we explore how teaching presence might be manifested.

Part II

Applying the framework

The goal of this section is to provide guidelines for practice. Here the principles associated with the application of e-learning are identified and discussed. These principles provide an understanding of the properties and potential of e-learning that go beyond tools and techniques. They provide the foundation of informed and adaptable practice that is applicable to a broad range of contexts and purposes.

Chapter 8

Guidelines for practice

Nothing has brought pedagogical theory into greater disrepute than the belief that it is identified with handing out to teachers recipes and models to be followed in teaching.

(Dewey 1916: 170)

Effective teaching requires more than a repertoire of techniques or recipes. The reality is that there is an abundance of craft 'know how' books offering guidance on how to conduct an e-learning experience. Such approaches do not provide a coherent perspective or understanding of the interplay between the collaborative (social) and constructivist (cognitive) nature of a proper teaching and learning transaction. Nor do they provide an appreciation of the elements and unique characteristics of the e-learning experience. As we expect students to be mindful of the discipline they are studying, we should also expect teachers to be pedagogically mindful of a meaningful and worthwhile learning experience.

To be sure, the approach advocated here is not simply that of a 'guide on the side.' The teacher, or if you wish, the facilitator, plays a key role throughout the e-learning experience – even when discourse and activities are controlled by the students. The teacher is an ever-present and key person, managing and monitoring the process. We suggest that teacher presence is a necessary part in both formal and non-formal learning contexts. There is always a need for a teacher or facilitator to structure, shape, and assess the learning experience if it is to be more than fortuitous learning.

In the first part of this book, we provided the theoretical framework that describes the principles and organization of an e-learning experience. Here, in Part II, we provide a pragmatic discussion of an e-learning experience. The discussion is embedded in the previous theoretical framework in order to provide a deeper understanding of the purposes and functions of various educational methods and techniques. There is an assumption as well with regard to the necessity to accommodate the inevitable cognitive and social development during an educational experience. Therefore, goals and methods must also evolve as the learning progresses. At the heart of this is the recognition of the relationship between learning activities and learning outcomes. Learning activities should be context dependent and congruent with intended outcomes.

LEARNING ACTIVITIES

Simple lists of learning activities or the latest trendy technique provide little rationale for selecting particular activities. The following classification (see Figure 8.1) identifies the four fundamental learning activities: listening, talking, reading, and writing. This figure helps us to understand the purposes and strengths of each learning activity. These activities are organized and understood from a cognitive or content perspective as well as from an organizational or transactional perspective.

For example, content has traditionally been assimilated largely through listening and reading. The counterpart to listening, that is, talking or discourse, is too often severely limited with the result that less emphasis is implicitly placed on the collaborative construction of meaning and confirmation of understanding. Similarly, from the individual reflective perspective, we see a bias towards reading but fewer opportunities to rigorously bring ideas together coherently through the writing process. Educationally, we appear to be emphasizing information acquisition while limiting opportunities for critical discourse and higher-order knowledge construction.

From an e-learning point of view, the bias shifts to reading and writing activities, which, traditionally, are concomitant with private-learning activities. This, of course, significantly changes in an e-learning context in that listening and talking are substituted with reading and writing. Reading and writing are both an individual and collaborative means of communication in an e-learning

	Exploratory (information acquisition)	Confirmatory (knowledge construction)
Group	LISTENING	TALKING
Individual	READING	WRITING

Figure 8.1 Learning activities

experience. Reading becomes both a means to acquire information as well as to 'listen' to the views of the teacher and students. Correspondingly, in an e-learning context, writing becomes the means to both construct meaning and communicate questions and ideas with the teacher and fellow students. With e-learning and computer conferencing, we listen by reading and talk by writing.

What place is there then for the traditional group activities of listening and talking? Are these activities simply abandoned in e-learning? If so, what do we lose educationally? It has been our experience, supported in the literature, that students very much value real-time verbal interaction. The question is how important are listening and talking activities and what is their function in the context of cognitive, social, and teaching presence?

It would appear that verbal dialogue may have an advantage in the early, exploratory phases of practical inquiry. However, there is perhaps a stronger connection between verbal discourse and social presence. Experience has shown that e-learning students very much seek out other students, either face-to-face or by phone. Real-time, sustained verbal discourse is of considerable advantage in establishing social, cognitive, and teaching presence, particularly in the early phase of an educational experience. Notwithstanding this, having recognized the inherent differences in synchronous verbal communication and asynchronous text-based communication, the discussion here focuses on facilitating an asynchronous e-learning experience. That is not to say that we will not address the advantages of preceding or following an e-learning experience with an opportunity to engage others in a face-to-face encounter.

Before turning specifically to e-learning guidelines, we need to reiterate that teacher–facilitators approach an educational e-learning experience as neither a 'sage on the stage' nor a 'guide on the side.' We believe that one is as biased as the other in approaching the design and delivery of an educational experience. However, considering the inherent complexity and challenges of an educational experience, there may be a place for either or both as the experience develops. An educational experience is properly composed of a teacher and student with a shared purpose but with different responsibilities. Contrary to what some contend (Collison *et al.* 2000), it is simply not true that the 'guide on the side' is most appropriate for facilitating an e-learning experience. Considerable emphasis must be placed on teaching presence.

Teaching–learning guidelines

We approach these practical guidelines from the perspective of teaching presence and its three dimensions: instructional management, facilitating discourse, and direct instruction. Within each of the three teaching presence dimensions we discuss issues of social and cognitive presence that the teaching function must address. Teaching presence encompasses more than the exchange of messages. In addition to the facilitation of critical discourse, it includes readings, exercises, Web explorations, and collaborative projects, to name a few. The first challenge is to consider which activities to include and how they will be integrated into a meaningful educational experience. Design and organization are the first elements of teaching presence and must be approached by concurrently considering both social and cognitive presence issues.

Design and organization

To begin with, we must appreciate that the roles of teacher and student in an e-learning transaction are both congruent with, and different from, their roles in a traditional face-to-face classroom experience. That is, as discussed in Chapter 2, the essential elements in approaching an educational experience in a collaborative, constructivist manner remain inviolable. At the same time, in terms of asynchronous text-based communication and the accessibility to resources, e-learning represents a paradigm shift in how the teaching and learning transaction plays out. It is to these issues and their practical implications that we turn our attention.

It is important to realize here, that the process of planning a quality e-learning experience is very likely to be more complex and time-consuming than planning a conventional classroom experience. Thinking through the structure, process, and evaluation aspects of an e-learning course raises special challenges. Simply put, expectations learned in a conventional classroom setting do not apply in an e-learning educational experience. The introduction and orientation will greatly influence sustained motivation and must, therefore, be carefully considered. These challenges also present opportunities to do things better educationally through more transparent teacher presence and modelling. For this reason, much of the success of the e-learning experience will depend on teacher responsibility for design and organization.

It is important to appreciate that, in a collaborative constructivist approach, design is not a rigid template that is imposed on the learning situation. The design must be inherently flexible and adaptable to unpredictable and individual learning needs as they arise. Design and redesign continue throughout the educational experience as collaboration and shared control introduce a creative element of uncertainty. This constructivist freedom with an educational purpose takes advantage of the great strength of e-learning and outlines a major advantage over prescriptive, self-instructional course packages. Curriculum must be relatively open and the teacher an active participant, not a spectator. Moreover, students must have an appropriate degree of control over the management and monitoring of their activities and learning. Responsibility and control must naturally evolve as the learner progresses socially and cognitively. This developmental theme is reflected in each of the subsequent sections on the design of social and cognitive presence. This helps us understand what kinds of activities and support are needed in progressive phases of learning.

From a design and organizational perspective, specific guidelines and suggestions for practice include:

1   establishing curriculum;
2   identifying resources;
3   defining clear expectations and goals (process and content);
4   addressing technological concerns;
5   structuring activities (collaborative and individual);
6   setting time-frames;
7   devising assessment processes and instruments; and
8   selecting media.

These must be considered in-depth both before and during the e-learning experience. During the design phase teachers must do their best to provide reasonable structure (goals, expectations) and anticipate as best they can the evolving needs of the students.

While specific design suggestions will follow, a comment about addressing technological concerns is appropriate here. It is easy to say that technology should be transparent, but this is an ideal, predicated on training and support. The transparency issue is compounded by the constant introduction of new media and standards. It may be a special challenge to provide technology training and support for students at a distance. While teaching in-service can often be done in face-to-face seminars and workshops, consideration should be given to on-line support through learning and knowledge management systems and communities of practice (see Chapter 10). For students, special efforts need to be made to have them become comfortable with the technology. Experience has shown that technology training will invariably require more time than is initially estimated. Greatest success is achieved where training is offered in stages and where new training is applied immediately.

Social presence

Because e-learning can be accompanied by a sense of aloneness, one of the first and most important challenges for the teacher is to establish social presence. It is crucial that each student feels welcomed and is given the reassurance that they are part of a community of learners. This sense of belonging provides group cohesion and the resulting security facilitates open communication, including the acceptability of expressing emotions. Social presence is essential in a collaborative learning experience and is a necessary precondition to establishing cognitive presence.

From a social-presence perspective it is helpful to understand the general developmental dynamics of groups. Even though groups do vary considerably in their cohesiveness and evolution, some insight into group dynamics can be useful in anticipating social conflicts or reduced motivation. There are several group development theories that essentially confirm that groups evolve in a relatively systematic manner. Perhaps the best known is that of Tuckman (1965) who postulates five stages: forming, storming, norming, performing, and adjourning. From an educational perspective Pratt (1981) simplifies this pattern to the beginning, middle, and ending phases that we will use to highlight social-presence issues.

In the initial phase, students must feel included if they are to form a cohesive community of inquiry. In the middle, or productive phase, there will inevitably be conflicts (storming) and the need for resolution (norming). It is difficult to predict when, and to what degree, the storming and norming process will manifest itself. One should be aware of this difficulty because the process might not surface in an overt and obvious way, but may still have a detrimental effect on open communication and critical discourse. If students are to take control and responsibility for their learning, then teachers must expect challenges and conflict. The key is to address these conflicts constructively with negotiation and respect. This conflict and resolution process may repeat itself throughout the productive phase. As groups bond, endings become important. Preparation for transition and emotional closure are issues that should be addressed (Pratt 1981). These dynamics provide the climate to establish cognitive presence.

Some conflict is inevitable and is not unhealthy if scepticism and critical reflection are to be encouraged. The challenge is to create trust but not discourage respectful dissent or criticism. Here, teachers can model the appropriate behaviour by opening themselves to challenges from students. Paralleling the characteristics of reflection and dialogue inherent in asynchronous e-learning, students must be separate but part of the community. That is, they must be allowed and encouraged to maintain cognitive independence to construct meaning while contributing to mutual understanding.

Preparation for the first session is important in any educational experience, but crucial in an e-learning context. In establishing social presence, paradoxically, the vehicle should be substantive educational concerns and issues. Certainly, special efforts must be made to allow participants to introduce themselves, but the first session should not be just a social event. It must be kept in mind that the purpose of establishing social presence is to support and enhance a sustained, critical community of inquiry. Through the use of chat rooms, collaborative assignments, and discourse associated with subject-related critical inquiry, students will gain trust over time. Establishing social presence is not a one-time activity.

While student motivation may initially be high, sustaining this motivation throughout the course of studies will, to a considerable extent, be a function of cohesion and collaboration. Consideration must be given to anticipating how to involve reluctant students as well as focus or limit contributions from over-enthusiastic participants. Not all students will feel comfortable in an e-learning environment, and all students will need to know the rules and etiquette. Here, clear expectations as to the length and frequency of contributions should be provided before the course begins. Although not all students need to participate at the same frequency as their peers, they should be made aware that they should stay in touch on a regular basis. Accommodation must be made for individual differences and this is why decisions regarding assigning grades based upon participation need to be made with care.

The great challenge for teachers in establishing social presence is setting the right tone at the right time. The right tone may range from nurturing and emotionally supportive to questioning and analytical. The tone of the conversation should correspond with cognitive presence issues and goals. At times the teacher may be a guide on the side (i.e., facilitator), at times a sage on the stage (i.e., direct instructor) – or, at other times, something in between in the role of an active moderator. All these roles require teaching presence with an educational goal in mind.

The first dimension of teaching presence, design and organization should build a special presence that establishes:

1 a feeling of trust and being welcomed;
2 a sense of belonging to a critical community;
3 a sense of control;
4 a sense of accomplishment;
5 a willingness to engage in discourse;
6 a conversational tone; and
7 a questioning attitude.

Cognitive presence

Ultimately the purpose of any educational experience is learning; but not just indiscriminate or fortuitous learning. The premise of this book is that e-learning is more than the undirected, unreflective exchange of opinions. Higher education places value on higher-order learning outcomes. The critical thinking process required to achieve these outcomes necessitates complex and sustained communication between and among the teacher and students. Analysis of the dialogic writing process (i.e., text-based discourse) in an e-learning environment has only recently begun to receive attention.

To provide insight specific to the learning process, we have focused on a community of inquiry and the cognitive processes associated with such a practical inquiry approach (see Chapter 3). Cognitive presence is created directly through the critical reflection and dialogue described by the practical inquiry model. The four phases of practical inquiry associated with cognitive presence are: 1) a triggering event and sense of puzzlement or dissonance; 2) exploring this issue or problem through gathering and exchanging relevant information; 3) integrating or making sense of this information by connecting the ideas in a meaningful way; and, 4) resolving the issue by applying and testing the ideas either directly or vicariously.

Although students will progress naturally through these phases, not all will do so at the same rate or, necessarily in a linear fashion, and this must be considered when designing and organizing an educational experience. The issues raised by this inherent individualism are further complicated by social presence considerations and group dynamic developments. At the start of a course of studies, presenting issues or problems and exploring them are often congruent with the forming stage of the group, both cognitively and socially. The transformation from the presenting and exploring stages to the integration and resolution stages of inquiry may be the most difficult, but the transition will be much easier if group cohesion and trust are strong. The teacher must consider whether students have socially and cognitively matured and entered a collaborative constructive (i.e., performing) phase before moving on to the integration and resolution phase. The division of the group into smaller groups for discussion can be very beneficial for establishing cognitive and social presence.

More specifically, associated with teaching presence is responsibility for designing a variety of appropriate learning activities congruent with the cognitive task. This may take the form of searching for information on the Web, facilitating critical discourse, structuring small group projects, or overseeing student presentations. Teaching presence during the design phase entails creating a rich but flexible choice of activities for specific goals and purposes. Regulating time on task is also an important function. Students must have time to reflect and make sense of the content, but they must also be challenged and must move on if interest and motivation are to be maintained.

In designing an effective educational experience, particular consideration should be given to the use and development of case-based studies. Case studies focus discussion from a real-world perspective that students can relate to. They can utilize small and large group discussions, encourage students to take responsibility for extracting meaning, and provide opportunities for students to moderate discussions. Used in these ways, case-based studies can provide the perfect context for the teacher to introduce an organizing framework and to add additional issues or ideas.

From a cognitive presence design perspective, two issues – content and assessment – stand out. First, if higher-order learning outcomes are really valued, then students must not be overloaded with excess content. Teachers can be very tempted with unlimited access to information on the Internet. The great risk in too much content is that, directly or indirectly, it sends the message that the goal is to assimilate information. Students must have time to reflect, make sense of the content, and share understanding with participants in the community of inquiry. Cognitive tasks will change, but the process of iterating between reflection and discourse is constant. With virtually unlimited access to information in e-learning, students must have considerable control in deciding when more information is required. The ability to decide whether more information is needed is part of becoming a critical thinker and learning how to learn.

Second, cognitive presence will be strongly influenced by assessment and grading. Simply put, assessment must be congruent with intended learning outcomes. If the educational goals are higher-order learning outcomes, then assignments and tests must assess this level of learning. It is not good enough to emphasize critical discourse when students will be tested and graded on information recall. The quality of discourse and participation will drop rapidly, and students will devote their limited time resources to activities that are rewarded – assimilation of information. This kind of incongruence creates frustration for all and limits the potential of e-learning. We do not need the power of e-learning to support a collaborative, constructivist educational experience if all we intend to do is transmit information.

Asynchronous communication inherently provides for both reflection (construct) and discourse (contribute). The challenge for the teacher is to know when to emphasize one or the other. At the beginning of a learning experience, considerable structure and support is required to establish cognitive presence. Beyond clear content goals, it may be extremely advantageous to provide a metacognitive map of practical inquiry so students have specific ideas of their responsibilities in constructing meaning and thus understand the hows and whys of the learning activities and tasks. It can be extremely valuable if students understand that, while content, issues, and problems, as well as considerable direction, may be provided to start, greater cognitive independence and responsibility will be expected as the course progresses.

Cognitive presence issues associated with design and organization include:

1 consideration of assessment of cognitive development and knowledge at the entry level;
2 organization and limitation of curriculum;
3 selection of appropriate learning activities;
4 provision of time for reflection;
5 integration of small discussion groups and sessions;
6 provision of opportunities to model and reflect upon the critical thinking process; and
7 design of higher-order learning assessment instruments.

Facilitating discourse

Discourse goes to the core of the e-learning experience in that interaction is where the strength of e-learning lies and is the essence of an educational experience as evidenced by a collaborative inquiry-based process. Facilitation of the learning experience is the greatest challenge facing teachers in an e-learning environment. Facilitating discourse for the purpose of constructing meaning and confirming understanding is more than being a guide on the side or a sage on the stage. To make it work first requires a climate that will precipitate and sustain participation and reflective discussion.

Social presence

Education is socially situated. The need for social presence is derivative of this fact. Social presence is essential to creating a community of inquiry that, in turn, is central to a higher-education learning experience. Education is more than transmitting and assimilating content. It is about reflection, questioning, critical analysis, and collaboratively testing ideas. These basic activities do not thrive in a group without personal affiliation or where expression is not open and risk free. A sense of isolation or of not being connected will not encourage or support critical inquiry, nor will it engender intrinsic interest and motivation resulting from a shared experience that provides acknowledgement and a sense of accomplishment. Without these affective elements, engaging students and realizing deep understanding and the cognitive attitudes and skills to sustain continuous learning, are much less than certain.

The real value-add for educational institutions is creating and sustaining the context of that learning experience. The foundation of that context is social presence and a special challenge in an e-learning experience. Finally, much of what constitutes good, collaborative, constructivist (i.e., deep and meaningful) approaches to learning in a conventional classroom is translatable to the e-learning context. Perhaps the main difference is the emphasis of certain principles due to the reliance on asynchronous, written communication of the e-learning medium.

A word of clarification is required before proceeding. It is very difficult to discuss social presence in the absence of cognitive presence. Social presence is intimately connected to cognitive presence in that the subject and purpose of much discourse is of a cognitive nature and focused on understanding a specific curriculum. For example, responding to an individual's message, or expressing agreement, adds to both social and cognitive presence. This cognitive interaction, so essential to collaborative–constructivist educational experience, is predicated on, and sustained by, the social relationships and cohesion of the group. Practical inquiry is an inseparable iteration between reflection and discourse; between private and public worlds. For this reason, social and cognitive presence elements are abstractions that are not sustained in practice. Therefore, while we focus first on social presence guidelines and suggestions, cognitive issues are ever present.

In addition to having students post short biographies, perhaps in the chat room, a good start to an e-learning course is to form the students into small groups and ask each group to identify questions they may have about content and process expectations. This not only creates a good opportunity for the teacher to set the right tone for critical inquiry by clarifying process concerns and negotiating course expectations, but it allows students to become familiar with other students and the technology. Through open communication, teachers can reveal their thought processes and thus make themselves more accessible to students. Although the teacher must remain professional, revealing aspects of one's academic qualifications and, to some extent, personal interests can contribute to a welcoming environment. Students must feel secure but discussion should be purposeful and cognitively challenging. For this reason, it needs to be made clear that purely social or personal exchanges are welcomed but are best conducted in the chat room or coffeehouse.

Suggestions to facilitate social presence and establish a community of inquiry are:

1 Acknowledge and welcome participants as they enter a discussion.
2 Be encouraging, gentle and supportive while directing discussion.
3 Project your personality as a teacher and allow students to get to know you as a person to the appropriate degree.
4 Suggest that students log-on at least three times per week.
5 Encourage students to acknowledge individuals when responding to specific contributions.
6 Laud contributions when appropriate.
7 Be conversational and not too formal in communications.
8 Encourage 'lurkers' to participate.
9 Express feelings but avoid flaming.
10 Be cautious using humour, at least until familiarity is achieved.
11 Encourage students to inform the teacher by e-mail of tensions or anxiety.

Cognitive presence

Cognitive presence is the heart of an educational experience. That is, creating and sustaining a community of inquiry where students are engaged in a collaborative and reflective process consisting of four phases (i.e., practical inquiry) which include: understanding an issue or problem; searching for relevant information; connecting and integrating information; and actively confirming the understanding. The focus here is managing the process and monitoring the depth of understanding. This involves facilitating and focusing the discourse, providing appropriate insights and information when needed, and seeking some common understanding or insight.

The first challenge from a cognitive perspective is getting the attention of the students and engaging them in meaningful discussions so essential to a successful e-learning experience. Depending on the learning objective and the subject matter, there are typically two ways to approach this. The first is to provide one or two intriguing questions along with some associated readings or a case study. The goal is to have the students define the key question or issue, find the relevant information, suggest some meaningful order, and agree on a resolution. Students may be expected to explore the WWW for additional relevant information that can be reported on and 'bookmarked' for future reference. Here, the teacher is very much a moderator and guide. This approach is inductive, with the emphasis on creating order. The second approach is more deductive in nature and is more appropriate with well-ordered or defined subject matter. The goal of this approach is to provide a model or framework (perhaps competing models) with the challenge to the students being to gain some depth of understanding by testing the application in contexts familiar to them.

The core element and task, however, is facilitating (initiating, sustaining, and summarizing) stimulating and meaningful discourse where students actively participate and take responsibility for making sense of the course content. To 'lecture' on-line is to negate the power and capability of e-learning and, most detrimentally, to turn students into passive receptors of information. Critical thinking is content specific and needs to be led by a facilitator with content as well as context expertise. That is, they must know their subject, but they must also know how to moderate critical discourse in a largely text-based asynchronous learning environment. Facilitating deep understanding necessitates questioning, searching for key concepts, making connections, injection of ideas or concepts, constructing frameworks, diagnosis of misconceptions, and reviewing and summarizing. This requires knowing when to give and take control, when to encourage student input, and when to inform.

Particular care must be exercised when moving the discourse to the later phases of practical inquiry. Perhaps due to the prevalent guide on the side approach, most e-learning educational experiences stall on the exploration phase and students are left to their own devices to create some order and resolve the dilemma – or not. Here the facilitator must have it clearly in mind that there will be resolution. This resolution may be predictable or it may not, depending on how well defined the subject matter is. In any case, there must be a relentless shaping of the discourse through the phases of practical inquiry. That does not mean that it is a simple linear process or that all phases are of equal importance. In practice, there will be iteration between and among phases and more time will be spent on some phases than others. For example, in less well-defined subject areas, the focus may be on exploration and integration. In well-defined subject areas, the focus may be largely on resolution.

One constant in this process is the need for discourse to stimulate and guide reflection. This is often best done in smaller groups and, therefore, is not a constraint in an e-learning context. These discussions should be private, unless the facilitator is invited in. Each group would be expected to report back to the full class. It is here that students are free to share their learning experiences and attempts to construct meaning. Together, they must formulate a mini-resolution to report back to the main group. Small group discussion may be used in all phases of practical inquiry to foster increased participation and develop responsibility to construct meaning.

This is also an opportunity to allow the students to moderate their own discussions. Student moderation can attenuate the authoritative influence of a teacher and encourage freer discussion. However, student moderated discussions lack a high degree of content expertise and, as a result, may not have the same ability to weave responses, add important information, and encourage critically reflective comments. Student moderation can be a very valuable experience for students but should have some guidance and oversight from the teacher (Rourke and Anderson, in press).

Encouraging students to monitor and manage their learning (i.e., to be self-directed), and thereby assuming responsibility and appropriate control of the learning experience, is the primary means of increasing metacognitive awareness and learning how to learn. Self-directed learning may well be the ultimate goal and measure of a quality educational experience. Therefore, considerable attention must be directed to increasing metacognitive awareness for higher-order learning outcomes to give students an idea of what critical thinking is and how it is done. Metacognitive awareness will provide a cognitive map of the complexities of critical thinking and discourse. It will be a guide for the teacher and students in progressing through the phases of critical thinking and discourse.

If students are to become lifelong learners, then they must be cognizant, not only of the goals, but also the purpose of learning activities. Through this awareness they can manage and monitor their activities and responses to make them congruent with the goals so they can begin to judge the success of their learning strategies and tactics. That is, students can begin to be aware of their thinking in order to regulate that thinking. This has to be the basis of critical questioning of one's self and others, and the foundation for the construction of meaningful and worthwhile knowledge. This awareness will go a long way to moving e-learning discussion beyond the early exploratory phase, where most e-learning discussions begin and end, and move the discourse on to the integration and application of new ideas and concepts.

Cognitive presence issues associated with facilitating discourse can be summarized as the need to:

1 focus discussion on key issues;
2 provide stimulating questions;
3 identify puzzling issues arising from responses;
4 challenge ideas and precipitate reflection;
5 moderate but not overly direct discussion;

6   test ideas theoretically or vicariously through application;
7   move on when discussion ebbs or has served its purpose; and
8   facilitate metacognitive awareness.

Direct instruction

The element of direct instruction is what clearly moves e-learning into an educational experience. It is the responsibility of the teacher to provide intellectual and pedagogic leadership. In higher education it is the teacher who is expected to set the intellectual climate, integrate research into the curriculum, model the characteristics of an inquisitive scholar, and initiate students into the nuances of the subject. Challenges will require direct intervention but with openness and integrity such that the student understands and has some choice in the transaction. Scaffolding (i.e., temporary support to develop higher cognitive skills) is an important component of most socially shared cognitive (i.e., collaborative constructivist) models of learning. This is not accomplished with a laissez-faire or passive collective approach.

Social presence

While on the surface it might seem that direct instruction would diminish social presence, it may well have just the opposite effect. First, let us reiterate that cognitive and social presence issues are inseparable from a teaching presence or educational transaction. Regardless of the cognitive challenges facing teachers and students, education is a collaborative and, therefore, social institution. Second, direct instruction will raise important social-presence considerations, demonstrating respect and relating to individuals or the group in a non-threatening way that leaves the feeling that the intervention is warranted. Students value input, but they must also be comfortable questioning or even challenging direct instruction. Motivation will always be influenced by social presence.

Motivation may be a problem if it is excessive. That is, a few students may dominate the discussion or intimidate others and prevent them from joining in. Here, direct intervention is required to encourage these students to listen to others and reflect upon larger chunks of the discourse. Direct intervention in this situation can also direct these more articulate and enthusiastic students to more constructive contributions.

In a highly interactive e-learning environment conflict will inevitably be an issue that needs to be managed. Direct intervention may be required if conflict interferes with class dynamics; however, students should be left to their own devices for minor squabbles. Over time, it can be expected that students will become increasingly socially and cognitively responsible. However, a single student can be destructive, to the point that open communication and discourse is effectively shut down. For the sake of group cohesion, very disruptive individuals will need to be confronted directly (via e-mail or phone) and exclusion considered.

Social presence issues associated with direct instruction are consistent with previous issues but must be approached with particular care as the comments are specific and often directed to individuals. Some suggestions are that you should:

1   shape discussion but don't dominate;
2   provide feedback with respect;
3   be constructive with corrective comments;
4   be open to negotiation and providing reasons;
5   deal with conflict quickly and privately.

Cognitive presence

The virtual presence of an instructor does not diminish the central role of teaching. One of the most ubiquitous functions of the teacher in any educational experience is responding to questions. In an educational context, this may require more than simply responding with another question in a Rogerian fashion. While not answering a question directly may be an appropriate technique in some situations, there are many more times when students need specific information or direction. They may need immediate answers for good cognitive reasons or because of time constraints and the need to expedite the educational process. After all, a formal educational experience is designed to provide both an efficient and effective approach that goes beyond a totally self-directed learning experience. There is, of course, a place for self-direction in both formal and informal learning experiences; however, in a formal educational environment, purpose and direction are guiding principles.

As a subject matter expert, explaining questions or clarifying misconceptions are not only constructive but important teaching responsibilities. Following from this, we strongly believe that a knowledgeable teacher has a responsibility to either frame the content or direct attention to specific concepts that could form the basis of an organizing framework. In this way, students have, or can construct, the schema that provide the foundation to facilitate continuous knowledge development. Regardless of the approach, this will necessitate appropriate intervention and, perhaps, direct instruction. The teacher's role goes beyond a neutral weaving of participants' contributions. It is to validate the framework or matrix where students' contributions may have some connection. It is then the responsibility of the students to reflect upon this and share their insights for confirmation or extension of the knowledge framework. This takes the learner beyond assimilating facts and information.

This direct instruction should be approached with the intent of taking the learner to higher-levels of cognitive development than they might have otherwise reached if they had operated independently. This means implementing, monitoring, and ending a range of learning activities and tasks that have specific learning objectives in mind. This requires direct instruction and solicitation of formative feedback. Higher-order learning depends on diagnosing misconceptions and on other means of formative evaluation that the teacher can use to intervene directly. These are crucial forms of direct instruction.

On the other hand, 'lecturing' and dictating values and viewpoints is a misuse of the technology and perhaps of the educational process. Too much direct instruction will most assuredly reduce interaction and limit critical reflection to the detriment of higher-order learning outcomes. Students must have the opportunity to contribute and develop their ideas. This requires establishing a delicate balance. At times, the situation calls for teacher participation, while at other times, the discussion may need direction or may need to be brought to a close. Direct instruction may be used to oblige students to look deeper into a topic.

Summarizing discourse segments and at the end of a course is also a crucial direct intervention. At these points it is often appropriate to extract key concepts and direct students to further learning challenges. This is important from both a cognitive and social presence perspective. Cognitively it can create a sense of accomplishment and provide an evaluation of the course. Socially it is an opportunity to have some closure and bid others farewell.

Cognitive presence issues associated with direct instruction can be summarized as the teacher's need to:

1   offer alternative ideas and perspectives for analysis and discussion;
2   respond directly to and elaborate on inquiries;
3   acknowledge uncertainty where it exists;
4   make connections among ideas;
5   construct frameworks;
6   summarize discussion and move the learning on; and
7   provide closure and foreshadow further study.

CONCLUSION

The focus in this chapter has been on teaching presence. In each of the three teaching presence dimensions, relevant issues of social and cognitive presence were discussed, and guidelines provided. These were illustrated in the developing case study provided at the end of each of the three sections. Organizing the discussion as we have is useful from the perspective of teaching responsibilities. However, it masks the challenges and issues of assessing and managing the learning process and outcomes. That is, considering the specific phases of practical inquiry or critical thinking as described in Chapter 6.

E-learning is a fast moving area of study and practice. For this reason, teachers need to be teaching scholars if they are to remain current. This represents a considerable task when combined with the additional workload of designing and delivering an e-learning educational experience. To compound the challenge, there are enormous administrative responsibilities and organizational issues that need also to be considered.

Chapter 9

Assessment and evaluation

> Assessment . . . is getting to know our students and the quality of their learning.
>
> (Ramsden 1992: 181)

In this chapter we examine the critical role played by evaluation and assessment in ensuring the quality of an e-learning experience. Although the terms evaluation and assessment have occasionally been used synonymously, we prefer to differentiate between the two terms. Assessment is used, in this text, to refer to the critical role in formal education of assessing students' attainment of educational objectives. Such assessment is, by necessity, multifaceted and can include: acquisition of skills and behavioural competencies; competency in applying cognitive skills, including capacity to apply critical and creative solutions to complex problems; and attitudinal demeanour, including capacity to be critical, supportive, enthusiastic, or sceptical as required in any given context. Generally, assessment occurs throughout the course, thereby providing formative feedback to students, and at the completion of the course providing summative information on learning accomplishments to both student and instructor.

On the other hand, evaluation is used to refer to the act of comparing a unit, course, or programme against some set of performance or outcome criteria. These criteria are often set by external agents or organizations, but the interests of the teacher and students are also driving forces within evaluation policies. Comprehensive evaluation includes measures of satisfaction, perceptions of learning, costing and cost benefits, and other criteria for programme success as defined by any or all relevant stakeholders or participants.

ASSESSING E-LEARNING

The importance of assessment in an educational experience cannot be overestimated. As Rowntree states, 'If we wish to discover the truth about an educational system, we must look into its assessment procedures' (1997: 1). This is one of the constants of the educational transaction. There is general consensus that assessment fundamentally shapes learning, particularly if we hope to approach learning in a deep and meaningful manner (Garrison and Archer 2000). That is, as discussed in Chapter 2, education should be a collaborative constructivist experience where understanding is developed within a critical community of inquiry. When it comes to the influence of assessment, e-learning is no exception.

The point has been made in the literature, as well as by the current authors, that distance education and e-learning is first and foremost about education; therefore, much of the theory and practice of quality education that has been developed over the years for campus-based education has direct relevance in designing assessment for e-learning. However, it is also true that the context within which education is practised affects design and practice. The distance education context is complicated by many factors, including: the mediation effects of the delivery and communication media; the lack of physical proximity and body language used for feedback in classrooms; the lack of instructor perception and control over the actual learning environment; the difficulty of authentication and privacy in distributed contexts; and the reduction of informal, after-class interaction in some forms of distance delivery. These differences create a markedly different set of 'hidden curriculum' (Anderson 2001) in e-learning that require a refocus and repurposing of classroom-developed assessment and evaluation.

Assessment is directly linked to effective teaching and learning by revealing understanding and achievement. For this to happen assessment must first be congruent with intended learning outcomes. For example, if the goal is to realize deep understanding of concepts and develop critical thinking abilities, these must be the focus of assessment – not the recall of fragmented bits of information. Therefore, assessment should diagnose misconceptions during the learning process and assess the quality of intended learning outcomes. This form of in-depth assessment is not for the faint of heart in any educational experience and it is no less challenging in an e-learning environment. However, the challenges can be mitigated through the effective use of the interactive and collaborative characteristics of e-learning.

Functions of assessment

In their seminal book, *How People Learn*, Donovan, Bransford, and Pellegrino (1999) cite 'assessment centered' as one of four critical characteristics of quality learning environments that are most conducive to higher-order learning. Assessment centred implies not only an end, or summative assessment of students' learning, but includes ongoing, frequent, and comprehensive formative assessment. Formative assessment provides feedback to students on their progress towards attaining these final goals. Dirks identifies five major uses for assessment:

1   Communicate the achievement status for students.
2   Provide self-evaluation information to the learner.
3   Student placement for educational paths or programmes (accreditation).
4   Motivate the learner.
5   Evaluate the effectiveness of instructional programmes.

(Dirks 1997: 3)

Examining each of these in turn, we first note that an educational experience (even in an e-learning context) is a social and a goal-orientated activity. From classic activity theory we know that humans generally behave rationally in order to accomplish specific goals. These goals are both socially and individually created and articulated. The formal class becomes a means by which learning is clearly articulated, measured, and the results are made explicitly available to the learner. From behavioural theory we know that humans are more likely to persevere when their purposeful activities are acknowledged and rewarded. Thus, assessment serves the fundamentally important role of providing feedback to students on their often considerable and challenging learning efforts.

Since knowledge is both externally and internally defined, assessment provides an integrating mechanism whereby external measures of learning accomplishments are matched with self-understanding of the learning process and self-assessment of accomplishments. Assessment also plays a critical function by providing external benchmarks that can be internalized. Such metacognition enhances learner self-awareness and better equips students for lifelong learning – an ultimate goal of all forms of higher education.

Formal higher education also plays a major role in credentialling professionals and certifying learning accomplishments. This filtering and quality-control function serves a useful purpose in acknowledging and rewarding competence and effort. Institutions of higher education take this credential function very seriously as it provides a necessary social function. Assessment is a fundamental mechanism of this credentialling process. Although there has been a great deal of criticism of credentialling, there is little doubt of its power to motivate learners and to grant prestige to successful learners and the institutions that control the accreditation, nor is there doubt of the general necessity for mechanisms that acknowledge and reward competence and accomplishment. The importance of the credentialling function accentuates the need for valid and reliable means of assessment.

Learners are also motivated by assessment activities. Many learners are adults who have had a great deal of experience with formal education assessment. They know how to study, how to decipher clues as to expectations (i.e., test-taking strategies), and the best students come to understand the relationship between quality assessments and the fundamental big ideas that ground knowledge and perspective in any discipline. Successful learners most often rely on assessment deadlines and activities to both pace and direct their learning efforts. Effective teachers use assessment activities strategically to motivate learners to engage successfully in productive learning activities.

Finally, we note that not only the learning context and the content are social artefacts, but that assessment itself is defined and created by institutions, teachers, and external credentialling or assessment organizations. Thus, the assessment strategy and activities chosen reflect both the explicit and hidden values and social norms of these individuals and the organizational structures of which they are a part. The teacher functions in most formal education contexts, as both a major actor in the learning transaction and a supposedly impartial evaluator of learning outcomes. This tension plays out in often confused human relationships in both face-to-face classrooms and in e-learning environments.

Having articulated the value of assessment in an educational learning experience, we now turn the discussion to the means by which assessment is best used in e-learning.

Assessing quality

Assessment must be linked to, and be congruent with, course objectives and activities if it is to produce intended outcomes. Many of us have had the experience of devising 'enrichment' or 'suggested activities' for students, only to realize that most students are too instrumentally focused and too busy with other commitments to undertake many uncredited extra tasks. However, throughout this book we have been arguing for the integration of cognitive, social, and teaching presence through participation in e-learning communities of inquiry – mostly supported through asynchronous text interaction. Given the necessity to relate effort to reward, we are forced to confront the question of how best to assess and reward student participation in e-learning conferences.

It is clear that students must perceive participation in e-learning discussions as a major component of the programme of studies. Thus, assessment activities must be integrated within the e-learning activities. However, teachers must also be careful not to overly structure the discourse through excessive evaluation and personal intervention. The social presence of the e-learning environment must be welcoming and positive enough that students willingly respond and support each other in cognitive growth – omnipresent assessment may lead students to conclude that the discussion is a 'teacher tool' and not one which they may create and modify to meet their individual and group educational needs.

Students perceive that their participation and resulting learning is related to the grades assigned for participation by the instructor. Jiang and Ting

(2000), in their report on college students studying via networked learning, find that students' perceived learning was significantly correlated to the percentage of grade weight assigned to participation and their resulting participation in discussion. Thus, it is important for teachers to value students' participation both informally, through frequent interaction themselves, and formally, through assessment. What types of assessment are most appropriate?

Assessing participation

Many e-learning teachers give student grades for participation on-line. Such reward for participation is unlike most classroom education, where it is common to provide very low or no marks for attendance and participation. In an e-learning educational experience, discourse is the prime component of the learning process. Palloff and Pratt (1999) argue that given this emphasis on the process of learning, participation in the process must be evaluated and appropriately rewarded. Most students are practical adults with much competition for their time, thus they are unlikely to participate in activities that are marginalized or viewed as supplemental to the course goals and assessment schema. Thus we see many e-learning courses offering as much as 40 to 50 per cent of the overall grade awarded for participation.

Many e-learning systems provide tracking features that allow teachers to monitor the number of log-ons and contributions to on-line forums. Thus, it is possible to quickly determine manifest data about student participation. However, tabulating the number of postings is not an accurate measure of student achievement or growth. We are also aware of a tendency in formal education for some students to adopt 'instrumental' attitudes towards learning, wherein they strategically focus only on teacher-defined outcomes. Like much quality educational research, quality student assessment is multifaceted and uses a variety of measuring devices. We next examine some of the means to assess participation and contribution.

The computer systems that underlie e-learning communications can fairly easily be used for quantitative analysis of student postings. Many of the familiar WWW delivery and development platforms such as WebCT and Blackboard automatically generate lists of numbers of student postings. These postings can then be viewed by date, author, topic, or other message tags. It is also relatively easy to have the machines tabulate the total length of an individual student's postings, but this practice may provide little useful data, because some students quote other students or external authors and others will rarely do so. The danger of using number-of-postings as an indicator of learning is that one is only measuring quantity, and not quality, of postings. Teachers who measure the number of postings, with few guidelines or feedback mechanisms for shaping the quality of the messages, usually succeed in getting participation, but it is unclear if this coerced participation influences the quality of the discourse and learning outcomes.

There are a variety of other ways in which computer communicated communication (CMC) messages can be quantifiably analysed, including quantitative content analysis and the relationship of messages to other messages in the thread. CMC postings can also be analysed for their relationship to other posting to illustrate which students have been initiating new postings and which are responding to other students. Finally, the science (and art) of data mining has progressed to the point where student activity on Web sites can be tracked and analysed from Web logs that record all activity at a particular site. (See Zaiane [2001] for a discussion of the challenges and opportunities of site mining.) However, most of these quantitative measurements are currently too labour intensive to be used outside of the researcher's laboratory. Although the quantity of student postings can be a useful guide to the instructor as formative feedback that identifies students who are not actively contributing, it is too rough a tool to be used for accurate assessment.

A more pedagogically sound assessment of student participation would result from a qualitative assessment of student participation, aided by e-learning course-management systems that display student postings in context. However, postings listed outside of the thread in which they were posted often rob the message of important context. Teachers who do undertake the task of assessing messages in context must be diligent to make their assessment criteria as visible as possible and to share these criteria at the beginning of the course. Curtin University provides a list of heuristics that a faculty member can use to guide their assessment of the quality of student participation. These guidelines ask the teacher to note if the student's postings:

- effectively encourage others to learn? To participate?
- contribute regularly, at each important stage of the unit?
- create a supportive and friendly environment in which to learn?
- take the initiative in responding to other students?
- seek to include other students in their discussions?
- successfully overcome any private barriers to participation?
- demonstrate a reflective approach to using CMC?
- use CMC in novel ways to increase their own and other students' learning?

(2001: introduction)

The challenge for teachers is be able to use these very broad guidelines in a manner that is objective and that is replicable enough to meet students' and institutional needs. While we argue that such a task is achievable, from a practical perspective, we are cautious about recommending such activities because the implications for teacher workload are huge. Since the ultimate goal of any formal education course is to induce learners to become cognizant of their own learning, we argue that it is possible to have students present their own evidence of meaningful participation in e-learning activities.

A number of authors have written about ways in which the student's own postings can be used as the basis for learning activities, student assessment, or both (Davie 1989; Paulsen 1995). Typically, students are asked, at the end of the course, to illustrate both their contributions and evidence of learning by composing a 'reflection piece' in which they quote from their own posting to the course. Students should be given guidance, such as the heuristics listed above, to help them extract quotations that illustrate their contributions. Obviously, students who have not participated will not be able to provide any transcript references from their own postings and, thus, will generally receive lower evaluation scores on the project. Alternatively, a student may still be able to show learning by selective extraction of relevant postings, thus providing room for the vicariously participating student (i.e., lurker).

A more structured set of heuristics that students can use to evaluate and document their own contributions to the discourse can be developed from the content analysis descriptors, indicators, and examples introduced previously. For example, students could be presented with the following summary of social-, cognitive-, and teaching-presence indicators and, using their postings as the unit of analysis, describe to which of the three categories their postings contribute most significantly.

Self-assessment of contributions can be further refined by having students undertake moderating functions during specific time frames during the course (Rourke and Anderson, in press). They can then be asked to demonstrate their contribution to the class and the discourse by quoting their contributions to teaching presence (such as summaries, welcoming comments, learning instigations, and other contributions).

ASSESSMENT ACTIVITIES

A good e-learning experience contains a balanced set of learning activities that work individually and together to induce engagement, discourse, and higher-order learning within the learning community. The e-learning environment can support a growing number of potential activities. Growing, because on-line technologies are continuing to evolve and support increased combinations of text and multimedia interaction that can occur in both synchronous and asynchronous time formats. Second, as a professional community, e-learning teachers are devising, testing, and sharing new learning activities.

Consistent with the increased emphasis on active learning and authentic assessment is increased use of portfolios of learner products, or artefacts, in e-learning. The construction of learning artefacts demonstrates knowledge acquisition in a very fundamental and obvious manner. Portfolio assessment also is congruent with assessment strategies that allow significant input from students into their own learning goals. Students can then embark on individual learning paths and demonstrate their accomplishment through the artefacts or evidence as demonstrated in their portfolio. The e-learning transcript can be used as one very useful component of the portfolio, and teachers can ask students to annotate, summarize, or otherwise add reflective metacognitive comments to their archived contributions.

Each of the activities and strategies employed to assess student learning has methodological and epistemological shortcomings. While using these strategies, we are attempting to measure complex domains of knowledge as they are instantiated in individual meaning contexts. Successfully undertaking these assessments is an immense challenge. Further, teachers are compelled to undertake these assessments in a transparent, reliable, and authentic manner that allows unsatisfied students or college administrators to challenge them. In order to reduce the error inherent in over-reliance on a single assessment activity, good teachers use a variety of assessments throughout the course. This variety should occur in the format of assessment: quizzes, short answer, longer articulated response, and term paper; in the degree of collaboration required, from individual to dyad to group assignments; in the role of assessor; from self to peer to teacher assessment to practicality of the assessment; and from assessing broad theoretical understanding to assessing very practical applications of new knowledge.

There is a growing interest in using problem-based learning (PBL) activities in e-learning education. PBL focuses learning by confronting students with ill-structured problems that mirror, as closely as possible, real issues and concerns from an authentic domain. They encourage students to be actively involved in their learning as problem solvers, as opposed to content receptors found in dissemination-based educational approaches. The teacher's role in PBL is, first, to construct authentic problems. These problems are based on curriculum or the domain of knowledge about which students are expected to gain knowledge and competency and should reflect the expertise and other learning potentials and characteristics of the learners. The teacher then seeks out, and makes available, an appropriate set of resources that students can use to find solutions to the problem.

During the PBL process, the teacher acts as a coach and a role model. Coaching functions include helping students to attack the problem at the correct level, assisting with structuring and documenting their tentative solutions, and helping students organize their learning activities in other ways. Of course, PBL inevitably includes false starts and trips down roads that do not lead to success – the teacher should not short circuit this important component of the problem-solving process. The teacher thus acts as a co-investigator in the problem solution, fading into the background as students' ability to solve problems without intervention grows.

Student assessment in PBL contexts is more challenging than assessing traditional educational outcomes in both campus and e-learning contexts. PBL attempts to induce deep levels of learning and to develop students' capacity and interest in self-directed learning – simple measurers of knowledge retention are not able to assess student growth in these important areas. Because of this, a variety of assessment activities are often built into PBL. These can include presentations in which students demonstrate or post their solutions to the problem, self and peer assessments in which students assess their own contributions and the contributions of other group members, and the development of concept maps that document problem solutions and the processes used to achieve those solutions.

PBL in an e-learning context is not significantly different from that which is orchestrated in a classroom setting. However, since most PBL activities are structured to allow group investigation, the needs for supporting group synchronization, document management, discussion, and task assignment must be supported. We have found that providing opportunities for synchronous activity through real-time audio (telephone) or text chat is important for students to efficiently plan and undertake group activities. In environments that are based solely on asynchronous interaction it is often difficult for groups to quickly allocate tasks and plan their problem-solving activities. We are also intrigued with the development of net-based collaborative environments such as Groove (www.groove.com) and Community Zero (http://www.communityzero.com/) that provide an environment for group-based collaborations that include calendars, text chat, documents management, and asynchronous discussion forums.

Database of learning products

The products of previous student work can be used very effectively in e-learning to provide exemplar models for current students. Remembering that a major function of assessment is to provide feedback for students on their own progress, providing copies of the work of past students, with marking comments and scores attached, is a powerful way to guide and enhance learning. E-learning provides both teachers and students with the means to effectively share this type of legacy learning content in a type of 'knowledge management' system. The development of systems to store, evaluate, and re-use educational objects is the most useful manifestation of knowledge management in a formal educational context. For example, the Merlot database (www.merlot.org) contains more then 5000 freely retrievable educational objects – many of which have been peer reviewed and contain comments on their use left by other teachers. It is most common to think of educational objects as being created and owned by teachers, but it is equally valid to consider collections of student work as objects that can be criticized, reviewed and augmented by subsequent classes of students. Thus, the ongoing learning community continuously builds knowledge, captures, and passes this knowledge forward to future classes.

Authenticating assessment

E-learning must cope with the problem of authenticating student learning when the student is not physically present. Or, in other words, how does one know that work or test results submitted were actually performed by the registered student. Recent interest in airline security will doubtless stimulate development of biometric identification systems such as retina scans or keystroke analysis, and these will eventually find their way into the practices of distance educators. However, in the immediate future, e-learning educators will continue to rely on the proven practices of more traditional distance-education systems such as the use of testing centres, using local invigilators, and combining distance with campus-based education. In many upper-level e-learning courses, reliance on objective – and especially time-sensitive – tests is minimalized and methods that rely on analysis and application of knowledge, such as essays and projects, are utilized more often. E-learning educators also make more extensive use of 'take home' exams, which not only circumvent problems of security and invigilation, but also provide more authentic tests of knowledge that mirror real-world tasks much more closely than timed tests and examinations.

Student participation

One of the inherent advantages of collaborative-based learning models is the capacity to discuss the critical role of assessment with students. In most cases of higher learning, e-learning can and should not be reduced to machine-marked assessment of teacher-defined assessment criteria. Rather, the inherent communications capacity of the Net can be used to allow students to comment upon, focus, and negotiate the assessment system so that it adequately reflects and guides their preferred learning objectives. Student control of the learning programme is central to effective adult learning. We have argued that, at its most fundamental level, 'control is concerned with the opportunity and ability to influence, direct, and determine decisions related to the educational process' (Garrison and Baynton 1987: 5) and that, 'if students are to have an expectation of control, they must have some choice over their educational goals' (Garrison 1997b: 28). This control must extend beyond choice of goals to choice of how these goals are assessed.

COURSE EVALUATION

Assessment of student learning is a key component of the evaluation of an on-line programme, but it is only one of the factors with which educators involved in e-learning are concerned. The e-learning context is complex and made up of many components. All these components must work together in a seamless fashion if quality, sustainable educational outcomes are to be produced. In the following section we provide a model of 'proactive assessment' developed by Roderick Sims (2001) to evaluate all the significant components of the e-learning context and intervention.

Proactive evaluation begins by determining the strategic intent of the e-learning programme. Being able to clearly identify why the particular educational programme has been developed and delivered on-line is critical to assessing its effectiveness. Traditionally, distance education courses have been offered in order to increase public access to formal education opportunities by spanning geographic or temporal distance. The same motivation lies behind e-learning, but the capabilities of e-learning speak to issues of quality as a function of interactive and collaborative capabilities. Institutions also attempt to use e-learning as a means to increase revenues, to increase or retain market share of students, and to enhance institutional or national recognition or prestige. E-learning has also been used as a means to acquire the skills essential to working in on-line environments. Obviously, knowledge of the strategic goals of e-learning is critical to establishing mechanisms for measuring the achievement of these goals. It should be noted that these goals are often hidden (Anderson 2001) and implicit; therefore, the first role of the educator–evaluator must be to explicate these hidden agendas.

The second element in proactive evaluation is to look closely at the content of the courses. Sims (2001) points out that content for any course exists along a continuum from the static content that is predetermined by the course developer–teacher, before any students are enrolled, to content that is totally constructed by the contributions of the students and teacher as the course progresses. Each component of this content must be congruent with other components such that a cohesive and easily understood package results. For example, writing style should be consistent and should match the reading level and the degree of familiarity with vocabulary appropriate to the average learner enrolled in the course. The content of the course material must be accurate and all authors should acknowledge any bias they bring to the discussion. While this seems to be a commonsense requirement it can become problematic as the learners contribute content.

The content should also be evaluated based on the ease with which it can be altered and amended to meet the needs of current and future students and teachers. Increasingly, content is re-used for a variety of educational applications, but the ease with which content can be adapted is directly related to its granularity. Content that is packed in large units, such as whole courses or long units, is often very difficult to re-use or customize if only pieces of the content are relevant to other users. In order for users to find and re-use content it must be identified and made accessible. To facilitate this, content can be 'tagged' with appropriate educational metatags (see http://cancore.org) and made accessible and retrievable by inclusion in a repository of educational objects such as those run at www.merlot.org or www.careo.org. Finally, both the process and the final output of appropriate quality control should also be evaluated.

Effective evaluation of e-learning material requires a close examination of the instructional design incorporated in the course. E-learning courses reflect the pedagogical biases and understandings of their creators. There are many examples of e-learning content that are based on instructivist designs but masquerading as constructivist designs. So, despite the protestations of some e-learning evangelists, we believe that an e-learning course should be consistent with the philosophy of the designers, and that it can reflect a variety of pedagogical assumptions about teaching and learning. Despite differences in design, every course should: be aligned with the prior experience and knowledge of the learners; provide pathways and sequencing that are coherent, clear, and complete; provide opportunities for discourse; and provide means by which both students and teachers can assess their learning and the expected outcomes; and the ways in which these outcomes are to be achieved should be clearly articulated.

The third area of proactive evaluation focuses on an examination of the interface design. An effective interface is easily mastered by participants and allows for presentation of content in a variety of formats including graphics, video, and sound. The design should also be based on a metaphor (such as a campus, building, desktop, filing system) that will help learners navigate among components of the course. The interface should also be customizable by both the students and the teacher to increase their comfort and the readability of the course. The cost of student access should be clearly articulated and built into the cost of the course so that no one is surprised by unanticipated expenses.

The fourth area of a proactive design looks at the amount of interactivity supported by the course. Traditionally, interactivity in distance education has been conceived as operating in three realms based on student involvement: student–student, student–teacher, and student–content. We have argued elsewhere that there are three additional types of interaction relevant to the e-learning context: teacher–content, teacher–teacher, and content–content (Anderson and Garrison 1997). Although it may seem rather anthropomorphic to discuss content interaction, we are convinced that the logic and intelligence that is currently being built into various autonomous agents will eventually give rise to a new type of content that is capable of updating itself and changing in response to interactions with teachers, learners and other content agents.

The fifth area revolves around evaluating the quality, quantity and thoroughness of the assessment of student learning. As discussed previously, assessment drives much learning behaviour and in many ways defines the course – at least as perceived by student participants. A proactive evaluation of the course looks closely at the assessment activities and notes how accurately they measure both the espoused and the hidden course objectives.

Most quality courses will have multiple forms of assessment, including assessment of both individual and group work. The means by which the assessment is authenticated against discipline or community norms is also a concern in this area of the evaluation.

The degree of student support forms the sixth focus of a proactive design. Since students are unique individuals, there are an infinite number of issues that may impede student learning during e-learning courses. To overcome these impediments, a variety of student support services must be available in conjunction with quality e-learning courses. These resources need to focus on the content (remedial activities for some and enrichment for other students), on technical issues (especially if the technology used for delivery support is sophisticated or complex), and on personal issues (including funding and various types of counselling support).

The final area of evaluation included in Sim's proactive evaluation relates to assessing the degree to which outcomes have been met. Are the learners satisfied with the courses? Are credentialling or accreditation organizations able to certify those who have successfully completed the courses? Are teachers satisfied with the work conditions and the workloads associated with the course? Are there mechanisms in place so that the course will be continuously improved during subsequent iterations? It may also be relevant to evaluate whether the course is affordable to students and profitable as a concern of institutional administrators. Finally, does achievement of the course outcomes really make a difference to individual students, their employers, and to the larger society?

CONCLUSION

As the breadth of the discussion above illustrates, judging the worth of an e-learning experience is a broad and complex topic that includes much more than merely assessing student performance outcomes and their perceptions of the value of the course. Rigorous evaluation is justified given the novelty of the development and delivery of e-learning. The next decade will see great development in the types and styles of e-learning. It is only through rigorous and systematic evaluation efforts that we will be able to develop our understanding of the many complex educational issues that rapid development will expose.

Chapter 10

Organizational issues

> Despite all the rhetoric to the contrary, institutions seem unable to take concerted steps toward the conception of the 'new university' that so many have insisted is needed to accommodate a full flowering of the technological and knowledge revolution.
>
> (Frye 2002: 10)

Institutions of higher education have purposely and seriously begun to position themselves with regard to e-learning. They have made serious efforts to move ahead from the public-relations rhetoric of suggesting innovation towards becoming leaders in drafting vision, policies, and goals with regard to e-learning. These institutions have begun to question and redefine their conceptions of what constitutes a quality learning experience in the context of an ubiquitous, mediated communications environment and have begun to understand where they really do add value. The answer as to what distinguishes institutions of higher education is increasingly being seen in terms of the context and process of learning (i.e., community of inquiry) and not access to content. By revisiting their core values and culture, these institutions are recognizing a need to change and are realizing that e-learning may be the catalyst and means to significantly enhance the scholarly culture and learning environment.

Expectations are changing, and there is little question that institutions of higher education are being transformed as a result of e-learning innovations. However, the question is how this transformation will be led and managed. Institutions face the challenge of developing a vision and strategic direction that will position them to move forward while not reducing their agility to adapt to new developments. Meeting this challenge demands insightful and resourceful organizational leadership. This is the focus of this chapter.

STRATEGIC INNOVATION

E-learning is not an experiment. It has moved into the mainstream of higher education and is beginning to be recognized as a strategic asset. There is also a growing recognition of the pressing need to address inherent deficiencies in higher education related to over-reliance on lectures and information dissemination in our current system. The effort of the Massachusetts Institute of Technology (Young 2001) to provide open access to the content of all its courses should cause higher-education providers to seriously question where they add value. The important implication is that the real value-add is not simply course content, but the quality of the learning experience. In short, the purpose of innovation must be the enhancement of the quality of the learning environment and learning outcomes. Competition will be on quality. Unfortunately, too little time and effort is being expended on understanding e-learning and how it can serve core values and enhance quality. Too much effort has been used to sustain the status quo and too little time has been given to developing strategies to enhance the quality of the learning experience. Before we can effect worthwhile change and innovation, institutions must create a vision of the desired end state and begin strategic planning from there.

It is a false choice, and not an option, to suggest that an institution is campus-based and, therefore, e-learning does not have to be considered. E-learning pervades, and will transform, all teaching and learning whether it is campus-based, distributed, or distance education. Moreover, it has the real potential to enhance the traditional values and ethos of higher education by fostering communities of learners and through integration of research into the curriculum. E-learning can substantially enhance these processes and outcomes. The challenge for institutions is to adopt what is, in the short term, a disruptive technology, in such a way that it enhances core values while positioning the institution for the demand and opportunity of innovative technology.

Whether we care to admit it or not, e-learning is a disruptive technology in traditional institutions of higher education because it threatens the sustaining technology – the lecture. Disruptive technologies are invariably a threat to established institutions and, in the longer term, the source of their demise (Christensen 1997). According to Christensen, disruptive technologies have caused dominant firms to fail because those firms have refused, for whatever reasons, to adapt to them. The challenge for these institutions is to transform themselves during periods of technological change. Such fundamental change is currently being experienced in higher education. It is becoming ever more evident that, when considering the many advantages of e-learning, its ability to facilitate an enhanced yet more convenient and, in many cases, less expensive educational approach, is not mere hyperbole.

The winning strategy is to find relatively low-risk niche areas in which the technology can be understood and incubated and where, if there are failures, they will come early and be less expensive. From a business perspective, Christensen suggests, the 'innovator's task is to ensure that this innovation . . . is taken seriously . . . without putting at risk the needs of present customers . . .' (1997: xxiv). This perspective makes perfect sense in an educational institution. When innovating e-learning, the legitimate needs of campus-based learners and the core values of the faculty and the institution must be recognized or the disruptive technology will be greatly resisted – even at the institution's own peril.

> Attention to new, disruptive technologies should not preclude sufficient attention being paid to the sustaining technologies that will allow the central core of the institution to maintain its favourable position in the marketplace.
>
> (Archer, Garrison, and Anderson 1999: 24)

Academic leadership has a very challenging balancing task that must begin with development of sound policy and ownership of the innovation.

Policy development

Many universities are making substantial, albeit fragmented, investments in e-learning but, because of the lack of a strategic direction and a coherent approach, there is little benefit or fundamental change. Concurrent with incubating e-learning as a disruptive technology, institutional policy must be developed to provide direction and to focus sufficient resources to facilitate what will be a long and difficult process – the transformation of the sustaining technologies and vested interests of a large institution.

Some of the topics that a policy document and strategic plan should include are:

1 Vision
   – understand background
   – define core values
   – describe strategic goals
2 Needs and risk assessment
   – identify issues
   – identify challenges
   – identify best practices
3 Educational principles and outcomes described
4 Implementation initiatives and strategy
   – link to institutional priorities
   – create a steering committee

- identify communities of practice
5 Infrastructure
   - design multimedia classrooms
   - describe administrative processes
6 Infostructure
   - design institutional connectivity
   - create a knowledge management system
   - provide digital content
   - create standards
7 Support services
   - provide professional development
   - provide learner support
8 Budget and resources
9 Research and development framework
10 Benchmarking
   - establish success criteria
   - assess progress
   - communicate direction and accomplishments

While space does not allow a thorough discussion of each of these points, there are several issues that must be addressed to ensure that an e-learning vision and strategic plan are effectively created and implemented. First, the vision and strategic plan must have a few attainable, key goals and initiatives that have the support of the institution's leaders. Second, there must be an e-learning leader who has access to, and influence with, senior leaders during the construction of institutional plans and budgets. Third, research is necessary to remain current and innovative. As the Report of the Web-Based Education Commission states, a research framework is imperative and must be 'built on a deeper understanding of how people learn, how new tools support and assess learning gains, [and] what kinds of organizational structures support these gains' (2001: iv). Finally, considerable effort must be given to communication in order to ensure that e-learning remains a priority, that successes are shared, and that support is sustained.

Lasting innovation does not occur from the top down nor does it grow from the bottom up. More often than not, effecting change is an iterative process where middle-level leaders who have the expertise and commitment, along with access to both senior management and the grass-roots, are in the best position to formulate realistic strategic direction and influence institutional leadership. The vision must have strategic and practical value and be seen to be an imperative. Moreover, for leadership to commit to this vision, they must see the potential benefits and be assured of success. With this commitment, policy and resources can be directed to the integration of e-learning. However, the implementation of an e-learning integration policy will require a technology integration plan and the strategic planning that such a policy implies.

A technology plan must first delineate a process of basic education aimed at raising awareness of the potential of e-learning if it is to get beyond the early adopters. Institutions must provide specific training and support to introduce the concepts of e-learning with its unique approaches if teachers are to rethink their approaches to course design and delivery. For many teachers, this will require a significant shift in basic beliefs about the teaching and learning process. At the same time, the necessary infrastructure must be put in place or all of this will be for nothing.

Infrastructure

It should be clear that a vision and strategic plan must be systemic. That is, it is not sufficient to select elements of the strategic plan in a fragmented or ad hoc manner. All the elements of the plan must be integrated in a coherent and timely manner.

The system and conceptual approach that will best integrate the essential elements of an e-learning culture is a learning-management system with communities of practice at its core. Knowledge- or learning-management concepts and tools can create an enabling environment and provide much of the functionality for e-learning. Upon reflection, this should be of little surprise when we realize that higher education is about creating knowledge as well as managing its preservation and dissemination. Knowledge management is a natural underpinning and powerful extension of e-learning.

Knowledge or learning management is the needed 'middle ware' that links repositories and the educational process. It is the infrastructure that will empower the communities of practice that will ultimately provide the buy-in and sustainability of e-learning. With the phenomenal increase in access to information, the question is, how do professors (and students) navigate and manage this chaotic sea of data, information, and knowledge? With the consideration that higher-education institutions are knowledge-intensive organizations, it is essential that they manage their knowledge resources. Moreover, these knowledge resources are key to a quality e-learning experience. Institutions need to take the lead in prototyping sustainable knowledge-management systems.

While the area of knowledge management is evolving, it basically supports the creation, capture, organization, and dissemination of data, information, and knowledge (explicit and implicit) within and across communities of practice with similar interests and needs. This set of practices for teaching and learning can be classified into three core activities: content management, course management, and pedagogical management (see Figure 10.1). Knowledge or learning management can provide the interoperability for all components to synergistically work together for the enhancement of e-learning.

Much work has been done with content management and building repositories of learning objects and with repurposing these objects for specific users.

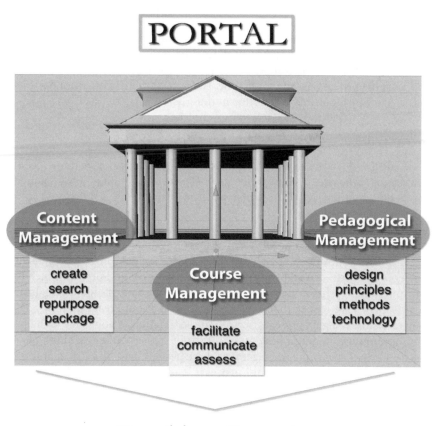

Figure 10.1 Knowledge management system

Considerable progress has also been made in terms of developing course-management systems such as Blackboard and WebCT. The development of support services to manage pedagogical and technical knowledge associated with designing and delivering quality e-learning experience is also required.

Equally important is the recognition and integration of communities of practice where teachers and students can manage and share information and knowledge with regard to curriculum, course management, and pedagogical processes. Knowledge management builds upon the foundation of a collaborative community of inquiry that involves both creation and application of knowledge (know-how embedded in the wisdom of practice). As Rosenberg states, the 'importance of community cannot be overstated' and its real power 'is that it creates opportunities for people to go beyond interaction with content to contributing information and sharing . . .' (2001: 80). That is, knowledge management encourages members of the community to consider new ideas, grow, and innovate.

To date, little emphasis has been placed on learning and pedagogical knowledge-management systems. Often knowledge repositories are under-utilized because they are not part of a community of practice. Moreover, such communities can contextualize and provide meaning to tacit and intuitive knowledge through the sharing of experiences that cannot be objectively codified. E-learning management must be able to serve specific user needs. Knowledge management can thrive only in a collaborative context where it can easily access, share, and repurpose knowledge.

Institutional leadership and expertise is required to implement a learning-management system that represents an emerging but transforming technology. Institutions must create a system that builds knowledge organically and is consistent with the values and culture of the institution. Therefore, the focus is on interaction and development within communities of inquiry and practice. The question is, what is the technology and infrastructure required to support communities of practice, which could be grown to support broader institutional needs?

Building upon communities of practice provides the best chance of changing faculty behaviour in the classroom for the better. Building upon personal and disciplinary interests through communities of practice enhances sustainability of a knowledge-management system. Concurrent with community building must be exploration and experimentation with platforms and tools that can integrate encoded knowledge while recognizing the dynamic socially situated nature of knowledge creation and application. To a large extent, the technology and tools exist. The need is for an institutional vision and strategic plan that will use them.

From an institutional perspective, it is also essential that a pilot project be designed that has every chance for sustainability and success, and that the prototypes developed in the pilot will have application across the institution. It is essential that the investment be made in a learning system that will serve the entire institution through access to a portal. For purposes of prototyping, it is very useful to strategically select communities of practice that are of high priority for, and are congruent with, institutional goals. That is, they must have strategic importance for the institution and be manageable in terms of size and focus.

It is important to ensure, before implementation, that the initiative is aligned with institutional goals and connected with those who have a direct interest in e-learning and knowledge-management systems. Key elements will include defining expected outcomes, working closely with other units, nurturing the communities, creating technological infrastructure, and assessing results. Some of the key goals to consider when building a knowledge-management system are to:

1   Promote communities of practice
    – conduct a needs assessment
    – providing for professional conversation
    – building a directory of expertise
2   Create repositories of
    – pedagogy; best practices
    – curriculum
    – assessment
    – learning technologies
3   Develop on-line knowledge links
4   Offer advisory services
5   Establish external access to others, partners
6   Determine technological solutions, capabilities
7   Construct a portal

As noted previously, to make a knowledge-management system work effectively, it must be local and personalized. A knowledge-management system and support network must be natural and responsive. That is, it must have a portal or gateway that can meet the needs of the users based on their interests and needs, ranging from accessing specific information just in time, to participating (i.e., contribute and question) in a community of practice to resolve more complex issues. A portal is a necessity for a mature, knowledge-management system and support network. Its users include both faculty and students, and its primary goal is enhanced learner outcomes.

As alluded to previously, institutional investment in e-learning and associated infrastructure will require not only the full commitment of senior administration but the leadership of a person with status and access. Successful innovation demands strong leadership.

LEADERSHIP

E-learning is at the centre of a transformation in teaching and learning in higher education. In times of fundamental change, successful transformation depends not only on vision, strategic planning, and infrastructure development, but also on strong, proactive leadership. In institutions of higher education, leadership is a crucial commodity.

There is a core set of leadership values and characteristics required to fully integrate e-learning into the institutional mainstream in higher education. The foundational values and personal virtues essential to leading the transformational process are integrity and openness. Successful leaders treat people with fairness, honesty, openness, and respect. These leadership qualities instil the confidence in others to provide the key information required to effect worthwhile change.

These values and virtues may be manifested in numerous ways. The characteristics we focus on here are vision, commitment, decisiveness, and the ability and willingness to recognize talent and give credit. First, such a leader must have a vision, and must press for it – a dream that recognizes and addresses the realities of larger societal changes and is consistent with the larger goals of the institution. This vision must then be translated into understandable and achievable strategic goals.

Next, the leader must show commitment to action and a willingness to make difficult decisions. Commitment to action reflects decisiveness. Decisiveness is a corollary to change and 'requires conviction, courage and action, often in the face of controversy and resistance' (Garrison 2001). It mediates vision and action. Decisiveness represents the courage to move forward with the expectation that adjustments will need to be made. The future can never be predicted and, consequently, surprises (and sometimes failures) will inevitably occur along the way. A strong leader will expect these setbacks, accept and learn from them, and move on.

While innovation is commonplace, true transformation occurs only rarely. Adopting e-learning in its full potential is a transformative process that requires a long-term commitment to overcome the inevitable resistance. Decisiveness is having the courage to make timely decisions, to seize opportunities, invariably without as much information or consultation as is desirable, or even prudent. A leader will listen and reflect very carefully but not be afraid to take the all-essential first step. Innovation and transformation do not emerge from consensus but, rather, consensus results from vision and decisive leadership. Leadership by consensus is an oxymoron.

Open communication and an ability to listen can identify and refine ideas but the value of collaboration must not be confused with the need for individual creativity, responsibility, and action. One of the great secrets of successful leadership is being able to recognize talent (or the lack thereof) and situate that talent appropriately. There is no substitute for raw talent. All it may take is a few key, dedicated and talented individuals in the right places to make things happen. This is particularly true in leading the adoption of e-learning and transforming learning in the organization.

CONCLUSION

In the coming together of the information era and the need for continuous learning, institutions must be prepared to focus greater attention on the strategic integration of e-learning. Institutions of higher education need to rediscover their roots and ideals. This may well require constructing and communicating the vision and strategic plan in the face of considerable resistance. To be successful, leaders must understand the dynamics of change and be prepared to start small but successfully. They have to recognize and incubate e-learning as a disruptive technology, while demonstrating how it can meet the challenges and demands of the knowledge era.

Chapter 11

Future directions

> if we want to see beyond the current horizon of scrapbook multimedia, it is important first to identify the essential properties of digital environments.
>
> (Murray 1997: 68)

Invariably, new media simply imitate old media without recognizing the unique characteristics of those media (McLuhan 1995). Now at the start of the twenty-first century, some thirty years after the advent of the desktop computer, we are just beginning to discover the unique multiplicative properties of e-learning. Those are the properties of e-learning that take it beyond imitating old technology and the additive novelty of computer-based media. The additive model is one that replicates the delivery of lectures over a computer and the Internet enhanced with multimedia analogues to the overheads of a lecture. This in no way recognizes the communicative freedom of e-learning.

PROPERTIES OF E-LEARNING

We are on the cusp of fully discovering the unique properties of e-learning and its impact on the educational system. The multiplicative communication properties of e-learning represent a qualitative shift in interactivity and discourse characterized first by asynchronous interaction and dynamic control of space and time. However, the true uniqueness of e-learning lies in its multidimensional forms of communication and interaction (i.e., simultaneous intimacy and distance; multirepresentational; hyper-searchable) that are truly multiplicative. Learners are able to assume control and directly influence outcomes.

The computer and the Internet are transforming all aspects of society. These technologies have become integrated into all aspects of our lives from e-mail to e-commerce. Although the integration of e-learning into business, government, and education has been subtler, it is migrating to the core of our social and economic life. The fact is that, in the fullness of e-learning's interactive complexity, rests a new expanded world of consciousness; a world with a different kind and quality of learning presence.

Technical systems tend to be seen as abstract from social reality. However, closer examination of, and experience with, e-learning's properties suggest the exact opposite. The fact is that technological artefacts and social relations are inextricably intertwined through the 'device and meaning, the technical and lifeworld' (Feenberg 1999: xii). It is how we understand and choose to use the technology that makes the difference qualitatively. Social interest can be enhanced by technology. The technical and lifeworld create a unique social and cognitive presence. The real potential of e-learning can only be found by revealing and freeing these unique properties. As Feenberg states: 'To be sure, technology may enframe and colonize; but it may also liberate repressed potentialities of the lifeworld that would otherwise have remained submerged' (1999: 222).

Younger students are more than aware of e-learning's liberating potential. Unfortunately, it has been the educational institutions that have enframed and repressed the unique communication and interactive potentialities of e-learning. It is the educators and administrators who must liberate themselves and who must climb the learning curve in terms of understanding and designing the kinds of dynamic learning environments that take full advantage of the potential of e-learning. Simply replicating face-to-face offerings, or transmitting volumes of information in an e-learning context, is doomed to failure.

Like bandwidth, content per se will have little direct value in the near future. If the trend continues, as it surely will, there will be virtually unlimited bandwidth and unlimited content storage at very little cost and, consequently, access to infinite content. The smart position for an educational institution is where many prestigious universities are positioning themselves now by adding value to the context or interactive side of the educational equation, creating quality-learning experiences that are engaging, relevant, and responsive. This is where e-learning will be centrally located. The discourse is shifting from the 'e,' or technology component, to the real issue – learning. That is, a quality-learning experience, regardless of communication mode or medium.

Educators can no longer sit on the sidelines without becoming irrelevant, without becoming extinct. Expectations are changing too rapidly. New models of e-learning are being invented at this moment. There are infinite possibilities and no single right way. Educators must assess their students' needs and find where and how they need to add value. More of the same, or doing the same thing more efficiently, misses the point. We do know that the role of educators is no longer simply presenting or providing access to content. Content is ubiquitous. The value-add of e-learning is creating a unique community of inquiry. It is in the design of an integrated social, cognitive, and teaching environment.

COMMUNITIES OF INQUIRY

Technology generally, and e-learning particularly, is a catalyst for communicative creativity and cognitive freedom. However, e-learning's flexible, controllable, and multidimensional interactivity, is grounded in a purposeful and highly engaged personal and public search for meaning and understanding. It is a common purpose that creates a viable community of inquiry and the means for the individual to construct meaningful knowledge. The essential ingredient in a functional community of inquiry is clarity and commitment of purpose. While all the technology may be present with the potential to provide an engaging, relevant, and responsive community, this does not just happen.

In an educational context, it is the teacher who takes the lead in defining goals, setting the limiting conditions of the inquiry, and providing the presence to regulate the interaction and development. However, there is also a great deal of unscripted interplay in an e-learning experience that provides for creativity and serendipity. Functional communities have a common purpose, but must also allow new meanings and understandings that recognize the uncertainty of knowledge to emerge. Each learner has the potential, through the power of their ideas, or through delegation, to provide teaching presence. Paradoxically, in a community of inquiry, the focus is the individual and the individual taking responsibility to construct meaning through the stimulation and dynamic of the group.

We will begin to see less reliance on lecture halls and increased integration of on-line discussion groups. There will be more simulations of real-world experiences that allow learners to take control and make sense of their decisions. E-learning must be constructed in such a way that learners can fully immerse themselves in the experience. This is not accomplished with a flow of information in one direction, regardless of whether it is to or from the individual. It is in the interaction that a special world of learning is created and where meaning is collaboratively constructed. It is where the teacher precipitates, monitors, and guides the dynamic interactions as they unfold, often unpredictably, resulting in wonderfully diverse learning outcomes. And it is where learners can repurpose activities to their own particular ends. This is the ultimate state of taking control and responsibility for one's learning. This is the uniqueness of e-learning.

The future is for those who are ready to assume control and responsibility for their learning; those who have acquired the critical thinking and learning abilities needed to cope with the 'too much information age.' Those who have learned to manage learning and create knowledge; those who are willing to act upon their learning and who are ready to shape change and not be the victims of it. The future of education is e-learning and a vision based on a deep understanding of its potential. It is simply not possible for educational institutions to ignore the technologies that are revolutionizing most other segments of society, to ignore developments that have seen the explosion of communities to serve business practice and personal interests. Why would education be immune from this?

DEVELOPMENTS ON THE NET

We conclude this book by examining features of the Net and related components of the education process that are driving significant change. Through this examination of the driving components, we hope to illuminate a future path for teachers and educational administrators that will help in the selection of the best Net-based tools and their application to important education and social problems. Because the Net has acquired a reputation of proving wrong those who proclaim to have discovered or invented the Next Big Thing, we hope this chapter will at least ensure that educators are there to assess, utilize, and improve the next Killer Application in both Net technology and educational application – whenever they arrive!

Drivers of change on the Net have been described by AT&IT Labs researcher Dana Moore (http://www.computer.org/internet/v4n1/moore. htm) as residing in three dimensions: volume, velocity, and variety, referred to as the 'three Vs' of the Internet Age (Moore 2000). He argues that each of these dimensions is expanding daily, explaining the speed and growing importance of the Net in many aspects of our social and economic interest. Within this ever-expanding landscape, we struggle continuously to find an all-important fourth V – value.

Volume

There is little doubt that the volume of education and training activity both on and off the Net is increasing around the globe. IDC, a US technology and market analysis firm, predicted in 2001 that the US corporate business-skills market would reach over $16.8 billion by 2004, with a five-year, compound, annual growth rate of 17 per cent. The reasons for the growth in demand for both training and longer-term education programming is directly related to rapid changes in technology, markets, and business processes – all of which demand continuous learning and retraining by all citizens. Further, there is strong growth in student numbers as a result of the baby-boom echo, coupled with the increasing numbers of adults enrolling in formal educational programming on a part-time basis. In addition, there are more adults returning to school on paid or unpaid sabbaticals or in response to forced or voluntary career changes. All of these factors lead to increased numbers of learners enrolling in training and education courses. Some of this demand is being met by traditional campus-based programming; however, a large and increasing percentage of courses are delivered via the Net. Corporate University Exchange predicted in 2000 that 40 per cent of corporate training funding will be expended on Net-based training by 2003.

There are many reasons for this continuing growth in enrolment in e-learning courses. Some students seek out e-learning courses for the same reasons that have always motivated distance education students, namely, demand for programming that is more accessible and that can be time shifted to meet the constraints of busy adult learners. But an even larger motivator is the growing evidence that certain kinds of e-learning courses can be delivered much more cost effectively than classroom-based instruction. (Though there are many variables that affect the cost of both campus and Net-based programming.) E-learning industry spokesperson, Brandon Hall, claimed in a 2001 *Fortune* magazine article that 'e-learning saves thirty to sixty per cent in costs over traditional classroom instruction.' While he provided few details to support the claim, there is a growing sense that e-learning is economically attractive, if only because it significantly reduces the costs of travel, accommodation, and replacement teachers, which account for more than 50 per cent of the cost of classroom instruction.

There is also evidence that the volume of Net-based programming for higher education is increasing as well. The Telecampus (www.telecampus. com) database, for example, lists over 40,000 on-line courses. A report by the Center for International Higher Education maintains that over the past decade, 'educational institutions, research centres, libraries, government agencies, commercial enterprises, advocacy groups, and a multitude of individuals have rushed to connect to the Internet' (Phipps 2000: 1). They further observe that an outcome of the increased connectivity to the Net has resulted in a corresponding increase of educational institutions that are integrating the Net in every aspect of their business, including course delivery.

For the first time in history, educators, trainers, and students are being presented with viable alternatives to classroom-based instruction in almost every field and discipline. We do not believe that classroom instruction will ever completely disappear. However, increasingly, both education and training will be structured to use expensive, classroom instruction only for the personal and highly intensive interaction that is only possible in face-to-face contexts. Much of the information transmission and routine dialogue will be supported both asynchronously and synchronously via the Net, to the greater convenience and accessibility of both students and instructors. Thus, the increased demand from lifelong learners and rapidly changing workplaces, coupled with increased sophistication and opportunity of Net-based education, will combine to propel large increases in the volume of Net-based educational programming.

Velocity

The search for the Holy Grail of computer-assisted learning has always focused on providing more choices to accommodate differences in learning styles and aptitudes, coupled with a quest for reducing the time required for effective learning to occur, thereby increasing the velocity of learning. While there is little definitive proof that computer-assisted instruction actually reduces student learning time, improves instructional design, increases student expertise, or unarguably improves the velocity of educational outcomes, we do not believe that we have reached a plateau from which higher-educational achievement and effectiveness is either unlikely or impossible. We expect continuing progress in the capacity for machines (led by the Net) to significantly improve a host of educational processes.

Of equal concern to educators is the time required to create and administer e-learning courses. Although it is difficult to accurately measure (much less predict) the cost of developing and effectively delivering e-learning, there is little doubt that the cost of quality education, delivered in any format, is significant. Sophisticated authoring packages and Web-based, learning-management systems are reducing the heavy time requirements demanded of early forms of computer-assisted learning. However, the time commitment to produce original Net-based, education programming remains a major impediment to more widespread adoption. A partial solution to this problem lies in more effective re-use of learning materials by larger numbers of teachers.

Two major developments – the creation of educational objects and the rapid and cost-effective distribution of these resources to both learners and teachers – promise to change the way, and the velocity, with which courses are produced. Educational objects are self-contained, digitized learning activities that are readily combined by educators into courses and learning modules (Downes 2000). Learning objects are at the correct level of granularity for adoption by a large number of educators. They are not as large as pre-packaged courses or programmes, which tend to threaten instructors who want or need to customize their courses to the unique needs of their students and to their own interests and competencies. Yet they are large enough to serve as self-contained learning activities and often contain assessment activities to measure learning results. Course development in the near future will consist of customizing internationalized sets of educational objects to best meet the unique localized needs of all students and teachers.

These learning objects are of little use, however, without a system of effective distribution. With no effective means for distribution, augmentation, or peer review, instructor-constructed objects too often languish on local servers. Educational object repositories are being created to overcome this challenge. The MERLOT repository at www.merlot.org now contains over 5000 educational objects, each of which is freely available on the Net for use by any educator. Further, the MERLOT consortium adds value to the objects by managing expert peer reviews and incorporating user comments, suggestions, and lesson plans to aid in effective use of the objects. Work on metadata standards led by the Instructional Media System (IMS) consortia (http://www.imsproject.com) and implemented in local repositories such as the Campus Alberta Repository of Educational Objects (http://www.careo. org) promise to increase the ease with which learning objects are catalogued, retrieved, and integrated into lessons and courses. Thus, we see the creation and distribution of educational objects being a major factor in increasing the velocity with which Net-based education is produced and distributed.

Variety

We are on the threshold of an explosion of media types available to educators on the Net. In the very near future educators will be provided with the opportunity to decide which communication format best meets their application needs, rather than which is most readily available. They will select from video, audio, animated, and text-based interaction. Although there remains a long and unresolved debate regarding the impact of the medium of delivery on educational attainment (Clark 1994, 2000; Kozma 1994), we do see the effect that the Net has on all aspects of our culture – including education. From commerce to religious celebration, from sports to stamp collecting, the Net fundamentally changes the economics, practice, and accessibility of most socially constructed institutions and practice. We find it highly unlikely that education will be immune from these disruptive changes.

We are also experiencing tremendous increases in the variety of ways in which information can be retrieved from the Net. Mobile devices, for instance, have spawned an interest in m-learning – the intersection of mobile computing and e-learning. M-learning promises an 'always on–always available' capacity to retrieve information, compute, and communicate and, thereby, be involved in learning activities 'anytime–anywhere.' These services will be especially useful for the mobile worker, the commuter, or anyone who operates from more than a single workplace.

The use of immersive learning environments, virtual reality simulations, and virtual laboratories will provide means for students to actively engage in complex learning scenarios via the Net. These technologies and others will change the way we think about e-learning, resulting in large increases in the variety of formats and types of learning activities available to teachers and students. However, we are reminded of Marshall McLuhan's observation that 'each form of transport not only carries, but translates and transforms the sender, the receiver and the message' (McLuhan 1995: 90). The and importance of education researchers in measuring and evaluating these transformations is immense. Through rigorous and reflective investigation, researchers will ensure that we add value, as well as variety, to Net-based education.

Value

There are many aspects of education and learning that are directly affected by the technological enhancement to human processes provided by the Net. One often thinks first of the capacity to find, store, and manipulate information. Since education is grounded in the systematic growth, management, and exploitation of information – thereby creating knowledge – tools that enhance the effectiveness or efficiency of the knowledge-management process will doubtlessly be used by educators to add value. In addition, the accessibility of the Net, with its promise of providing quality educational experiences 'anywhere–anytime' is also a significant value addition to the education process.

However, the real benefit relates not to ease of acquisition or manipulation of information, nor to increasing access to educational programming. The greatest benefit of the Net for education is its capacity to support the social construction of new knowledge and its validation and enhancement by participants spread around the world and across temporal space. That is, the value-add is quality. Access is a given; the issue and challenge is adding quality to access. This is the distinguishing property of e-learning and where it is changing how educators approach teaching and learning and has the greatest potential in enhancing the quality of educational outcomes.

For teachers and learners, this social world of thinking, learning, and acting has opened to the Net-based media in unique ways and has profoundly altered the nature of communications in educational contexts. We do not argue that Net-based interaction, in any of its formats – from synchronous to asynchronous or from full resolution video to text-based discussion – offers a best way to support education. But we do contend that no single mode of human communication, including the pre-Net standard of campus-based education, offers such educational perfection. Rather, the Net adds true value to education by providing both quality resources for independent study combined with a capacity for interactive learning. The instructor's toolkit has been augmented tremendously and the wise selection of Net-based tools from this kit will add significant value to both distance and campus-based education.

CONCLUSION

E-learning is distinguished, in a paradigmatic sense, from what went before. It represents a new 'learning ecology.' This is not just another add-on, but a technology that is transforming our educational institutions and how we conceptualize and experience teaching and learning. The challenge for twenty-first-century educators is to create a purposeful community of inquiry that integrates social, cognitive, and teaching presence in a way that will take full advantage of the unique properties of e-learning; those interactive properties that take learning well beyond the lecture hall and information assimilation. These properties of e-learning are capable of creating a community of inquiry that is independent of time and space and with the combination of interactive and reflective characteristics that can stimulate and facilitate a level of higher-order learning unimaginable to date.

We are just beginning the journey of discovery with regard to the uniqueness of e-learning. With this survey, we have attempted to provide a large-scale map of the territory and identify the key features of the landscape as we all embark on this exploration. The transcendent feature of this territory is a community of inquiry consisting of three structural elements. Those who are open to seeing things differently will recognize that the vehicle itself – the 'e' element – will alter what we see and, therefore, direct the course of the journey as we move into this uncharted territory. As educators experience new possibilities, and learners demand more than just information or content (as they are beginning to), then we will see e-learning being used in very different and very exciting ways. Clearly, we must see things in new ways and build new communities of learning along the way. However, we must also be aware of our educational ideals. Through these diverse perspectives and communities, we will reveal the unique properties of e-learning.

Appendix A

When we began the research programme that led to the creation of this book, we had a hunch that a great deal could be learned by systematic analysis of the written transcripts created during courses delivered via computer-mediated communications (CMC). Like all pragmatic researchers, we turned first to the extant research literature to learn from the experience of those who have gone before us. We found a great deal of interest in computer-mediated conferencing and its applications in education, but we were both surprised and disappointed at the few large-scale or systematic attempts at deriving knowledge from the transcripts. In order both to inform ourselves and to organize the various methodological issues that confronted us, we wrote a paper on the methodology, and reviewed the nineteen studies of content analysis of educational CMC that we had found. We have reproduced that article here as Appendix B. Our own experiences and feedback received from readers suggest that this article portrays many of the issues and points to solutions of value for future analysts.

In the paper, we focused on our first major concern, which was to develop tools that produced reliable results with different coders. We were disappointed at how many of the research reports we surveyed ignored or compromised the necessity to clearly report the means and the degree of reliability attained by their analysis tools and techniques. Thus a major focus of the paper was to find a means to calculate, improve, and document high levels of reliability.

Later in our research programme, our focus turned to issues of validity. How do we prove that the indicators we were counting did in fact accurately indicate the level of social, cognitive, and teaching presence experienced in the educational experience? Validity, unlike reliability, is not a construct amenable to numeric calculation, but rather consists of numerous facets – each of which is used to build a case proving that the data gleaned from the analysis of the transcripts is a valid reflection of the construct under investigation. Trochim (2000) defines the veracity by which a broad conceptual category is operationalized as construct validity. He lists the many different means by which construct validity can be built, including means by which the concept was translated into operational terms that he calls face and content validity, and a second group that shows how the inferences from these operationalizations perform in a congruent fashion to that expected of them. These latter groups are referred to as predictive, concurrent, convergent, and discriminative validity.

The extent of effort necessary to claim construct validity depends upon the nature of the construct and upon the variables used in its operationalization. For example, claims that the number of words per posting is a valid indicator of contribution have considerable face validity and thus little further effort would be needed. However, further evidence would be required to validly claim that the number of words posted revealed the amount of time spent on-line (subjects type at different rates), commitment to the course (a subject who types a great deal may not necessarily be reading the contributions of others), enjoyment, satisfaction, or especially the extent of learning achieved during the course. Construct validity gets more difficult as the construct under investigation becomes more complex and the indicators used to operationalize that construct are more latent. For example, making a case that a high incidence of supported argumentation in the transcript represents high levels of critical thinking requires face and content validity – proof that argumentation is theoretically and practically associated with critical thinking. Further, we would need to be convinced of its criteria-related validity by evidence such as results that show students with high scores of argument used, score higher on other tests of critical thinking, and that students who do not use argumentation score less well on such tests.

In our later work we used a variety of measures to triangulate the outcomes of the content analysis in attempts to build a case for congruent validity with the latent constructs, which we chose to study. For example, we conducted individual and focus group interviews, did weekly on-line surveys to test student perceptions of the construct that we would later measure in the transcript and shared our results with student subjects in attempts to get feedback as to the accuracy of our interpretations. We also checked our results against our theoretical model and the results of content analysis of other researchers, thereby defending the case for face and content validity. How well we built that case is open to question since we are dealing with complicated constructs and transcripts that give us only a trace of the cognition that happens in the hidden recesses of the student's mind. Bereiter and Scardemalia have argued:

> Knowledge telling and knowledge transforming refer to mental processes by which texts are composed, not to texts themselves. You cannot tell by reading this chapter whether we have engaged in problem-solving and knowledge-transforming operations while writing it or whether we have simply written down content that was already stored in memory in more or less the form presented here.
>
> (1987: 13)

This seems to suggest that establishing construct validity for cognitive and social constructs through analysis of transcripts is impossible. However, we argue that the transcript, like the tip of an iceberg, is not the whole structure of the iceberg, nor do the transcripts reveal all of the social and cognitive engagement during the course. But, through careful and systematic examination of these tracings, we believe we can make valid inferences about the social and cognitive presence – components of which will always be hidden from investigators – though we caution that one should not assume that the use of transcript analysis instruments, especially those newly created by the investigators themselves, are by themselves capable of proving a strong sense of construct validity. All instruments, and especially those that have not been extensively used in related domains, should be verified through a number of tests of validity.

Appendix B reproduces the methodological paper we published in 2000 in the *International Journal of Artificial Intelligence in Education*, 11, 3.

Appendix B

Methodological Issues in the Content Analysis of Computer Conference Transcripts

LIAM ROURKE

TERRY ANDERSON

D. R. GARRISON

WALTER ARCHER

ABSTRACT

This paper discusses the potential and the methodological challenges of analysing computer conference transcripts using quantitative content analysis. The paper is divided into six sections, which discuss: criteria for content analysis, research designs, types of content, units of analysis, ethical issues, and software to aid analysis. The discussion is supported with a survey of nineteen commonly referenced studies published during the last decade. The paper is designed to assist researchers in using content analysis to further the understanding of teaching and learning using computer conferencing.

Methodological Issues in the Content Analysis of Computer Conference Transcripts

SCENARIO

Professor Jones has just completed her first university course delivered entirely on-line. The 13-week semester class has left Jones in a state of mild exhaustion. However, the course is finished, the marks have been assigned, and now, thinks Jones, time for some reflection, analysis and perhaps a publishable paper. Jones smiles, confident in the knowledge that the complete transcript of messages exchanged during the course has been captured in machine-readable format. She feels that this accessible data will confirm her hypothesis that students in the on-line course had engaged in much higher levels of discourse and discussion than any she had experienced in ten years of face-to-face instruction. Further, she is interested in investigating the impact of the collaborative learning activity that she instituted in the middle of the course.

Jones is quickly disappointed. The 13-week discussion generated 950 messages. Merely reading them takes her four days. Attempts at cutting and pasting illustrations of higher level thinking into a word processor, have resulted in a hodge-podge of decontextualized quotations, each disparate enough to have Professor Jones questioning her own definitions of higher order thinking. Realizing that the analysis is going nowhere, Professor Jones goes back to the literature and finds a set of criteria laid down by an expert in the field that define the broad areas of thinking skills she sees being developed in the transcripts. Heartened, but now running out of time Professor Jones hires two graduate students to review the messages and identify the incidents of higher order thinking as defined by the expert. Two weeks later, the students report their results: not only have they failed to agree on 70% of the categorizations, but one student has identified 2032 incidents in the transcript, while the other has found only 635 incidents. To add to her misery, Professor Jones also learns that her university's ethics committee, concerned with the large increase in use of computer conferencing for credit courses, has ruled that without informed consent from students, her analysis does not conform with the guidelines of the university's ethical research policy. Feeling overwhelmed and depressed, Professor Jones returns to the educational literature once again, only to find that most of the methodological issues she has been dealing with have not been addressed by major researchers in the field. She also finds that there is no coherent, long-term tradition of researchers who have resolved the methodological problems inherent in the analysis of transcripts of text-based computer conferences.

This paper is written for the Professor Jones's of the world, hoping that it will help them to release the educational treasures that we believe are locked in the transcripts that document learning in the on-line environment.

The capacity of computer conferencing to support interaction among participants while providing for temporal and spatial independence creates a unique and valuable environment for distance, distributed, and lifelong learning applications. Additionally, the automatically recorded and machine-readable data generated by this technology offers a compelling source of data for educational researchers and software developers. This paper surveys the efforts of researchers to extract meaning from this data using a research technique called *quantitative content analysis*. Quantitative content analysis is 'a research technique for the objective, systematic, quantitative description of the manifest content of communication' (Berelson, 1952, p. 519). Despite the potential of this technique, researchers who have used it have described it as difficult, frustrating, and time-consuming. Very few have published results derived from a second content analysis.

This paper is, therefore, not a meta-analysis of results, but rather an examination of the issues related to the application of this research technique. The intent is to document the evolution of content analysis as it has been used by us and others to analyze transcripts of asynchronous, text-based, computer conferencing in educational settings. These modifiers 'asynchronous,' 'text-based,' and 'educational' provide a definitive focus for our survey. Unfortunately, this prohibits the discussion of some excellent content analysis studies; however, we feel that the use of conferencing in formal education is unique, and that the corpus of studies in this domain is sufficiently large to justify a focal review. We hope that the results of our review and commentary will facilitate the larger goal of improving the quality of teaching and learning through use of this medium.

This paper explores six fundamental issues of content analysis through reference to 19 influential content studies published over the last decade (see Table B.1). The first section examines three criteria of quantitative content analysis – objectivity, reliability, and systematic consistency. The second section contrasts the two most common research designs–descriptive and experimental. The third section distinguishes between manifest content and latent content, and the fourth section examines the process of transforming transcripts into units of data. The fifth and sixth sections discuss software packages that facilitate content analysis and ethical issues such as informed

Table B.1 Survey of nineteen computer-mediated communication content analysis studies

Study	Unit of analysis	Variables investigated	Reliability	Research design
Ahern, Peck, and Laycock (1992)	Message	Interaction Complexity of response	Percentage agreement	Descriptive Experimental
Blanchette (1999)	Thematic	Linguistic variation Participation Discussion themes	Not reported	Descriptive Quasi-experimental
Bullen (1998)	Thematic	Participation Critical thinking	Not reported	Descriptive
Craig *et al.* (2000)	Proposition	Student question type	Percentage agreement	Experimental
Fahy *et al.* (2000)	Sentence	Interaction Participation Critical thinking	Percentage agreement	Descriptive
Garrison, Anderson, and Archer (2000b)	Message	Critical thinking	Cohen's kappa	Descriptive
Hara, Bonk, and Angeli (2000)	Paragraph	Participation Interaction Social, cognitive, meta-cognitive elements	Percentage agreement Coder stability	Descriptive
Henri (1991)	Thematic	Participation Interaction Social, cognitive, meta-cognitive elements	Not reported	Descriptive
Hillman (1999)	Sentence	Patterns of interaction	Cohen's kappa	Descriptive
Howell-Richardson and Mellar (1996)	Illocutionary act	Participation Illocutionary properties Focus (group/task)	Not reported	Descriptive Quasi-experimental
Kanuka and Anderson (1998) Anderson and Kanuka (1997)	Thematic	Collaborative knowledge construction	Not reported	Descriptive
Marttunen (1997, 1998)	Message	Levels of argumentation/ counter argumentation	Reliability coefficient	Descriptive Quasi-experimental

Table B.1 (continued)

Study	Unit of analysis	Variables investigated	Reliability	Research design

McDonald (1998)	Thematic	Participation
		Interaction
		Group development
		Social, cognitive,
		   metacognitive
		   elements
			Cohen's kappa	Descriptive

Mower (1996)	Message	Interaction Topics	[a]Percentage agreement after discussion	Descriptive
Newman, Webb, and Cochrane (1995)	Thematic	Critical thinking	Percentage agreement after discussion	Descriptive
Rourke et al. (in press)	Thematic	Social interaction	Percentage agreement	Descriptive

Weiss and Morrison (1998)	Thematic and Message	Critical thinking
		Understanding/
		   correcting
		   misunderstandings
		Emotion
			Percentage agreement after discussion	Descriptive

Zhu (1996)	Thematic	Interaction Participation Participant roles Knowledge construction	Not reported	Descriptive

Note
Units of analysis for studies in which participation was described quantitatively are not documented in the table. Routinely, the units of analysis for this measure are number of words, messages, or both.
a Percentage agreement after discussion refers to reliability figures that were obtained through discussion between coders.

consent. The objective of this paper is to provide subsequent researchers with a privileged starting point for their content analysis studies and to contribute to the refinement of this powerful technique.

CRITERIA OF QUANTITATIVE CONTENT ANALYSIS

Quantitative content analysis can be reduced to four essential steps. Once researchers have a construct they wish to examine, the first step is to identify representative samples of the communication they wish to study. In traditional education studies, this has typically involved making audio or video recordings of classroom interaction between students and teachers, and then transcribing these recordings in preparation for analysis (Flanders, 1970; Sinclair and Coulthard, 1975). In computer-mediated communication (CMC) research, this intermediate step is unnecessary because the bulk of current computer conferencing communication is text-based in machine-readable form. Thus, analysis begins with the compilation of selections of transcripts or entire transcripts into text files. The second step involves creating a protocol for identifying and categorizing the target variable(s), and training coders to use this protocol. After a transcript has been coded, the coders' decisions are compared for reliability, and their data is analyzed either to describe the target variable(s), or to identify relationships between variables. The extent to which the resulting descriptions or relationships are valid will depend largely on four criteria discussed in the next subsections–objectivity, reliability, replicability, and systematic coherence.

Objectivity

Berelson (1952) stipulates that content analysis is an objective technique. In the context of content analysis, *objective* refers to the extent to which categorization of sections of transcripts is subject to influence by the coders. This technique, perhaps more so than any other quantitative technique, is susceptible to the infiltration of subjectivity and interpretive bias. Mower's (1996) candid discussion of reliability is illustrative:

> In instances of disagreement, [rater 1] agreed that [rater 2's] evaluation could be correct. In other instances of disagreement, it was determined that remarks could fit into either one of two categories depending upon the [rater's] interpretation. It was concluded that sometimes, subjective judgment was involved in assigning some topics to categories.
>
> (Mower, 1996, p. 220)

Mower's frankness reveals a pervasive issue in content analysis studies. While some amount of subjectivity may be unavoidable in coding transcripts, a quantitative study should not conclude with an admission that objectivity and reliability have not been achieved. Rather, the discovery of an excessive degree of subjectivity should signal to the research team that further refinement is needed in category definition or coding protocol.

Reliability

The primary test of objectivity in content studies is *interrater reliability*, defined as the extent to which different coders, each coding the same content, come to the same coding decisions. Potter and Levine-Donnerstein (1999) regard reliability data as an important part of content reports and offer the following advice: 'If content analysts cannot demonstrate strong reliability for their findings, then people who want to apply these findings should be wary of developing implementations' (p. 258). Of the 19 published studies in our sample, only ten reported reliability data (see Table B.1).

The simplest and most common method of reporting interrater reliability is the percent agreement statistic. This statistic reflects the number of agreements per total number of coding decisions. Holsti's (1969) coefficient of reliability (CR) provides a formula for calculating percent agreement:

$$CR = 2m / (n_1 + n_2)$$
Where: m = the number of coding decisions upon which the two coders agree
n_1 = number of coding decisions made by rater 1
n_2 = number of coding decisions made by rater 2

Many statisticians characterize interjudge agreement as inadequate because it does not account for chance agreement among raters (Capozzoli, McSweeney, and Sinha, 1999). Three of the studies in our sample used the *Cohen's kappa* (k) statistic to determine reliability. Cohen's kappa is a chance-corrected measure of interrater reliability that assumes two raters, n cases, and m mutually exclusive and exhaustive nominal categories (Capozzoli, McSweeney, and Sinha, 1999). The formula for calculating kappa is:

$$k = (F_o - F_c) / (N - F_c)$$
Where: N = the total number of judgements made by each coder
F_o = the number of judgements on which the coders agree
F_c = the number of judgements for which agreement is expected by chance.

In Cohen's (1960) original formula, agreement by chance is calculated in four steps. Researchers begin by counting the number of times a category of a coding scheme is used by the coders. Then, this figure is converted to a percentage of all coding decisions. Finally, this percentage is squared, and the squared percentages for all categoies are summed (see Capozzoli, McSweeney, and Sinha, 1999; Cohen, 1960; and Potter and Levine-Donnerstein, 1999 for further discussion).

Although kappa is a powerful measure of interrater reliability, some authors have argued that it is overly conservative (Potter and Levine-Donnerstein, 1999). This is particularly true with coding protocols that include several categories, thereby making the possibility of chance agreement negligible. Further, as Hagelin (1999) suggests, 'factors such as the number of observations, the number of categories, and the distribution of the data influence the kappa values in such a way as to make interrater agreement difficult to interpret' (p. 314).

The exact level of interrater reliability that must be achieved has not been clearly established. For Cohen's kappa, Capozzoli, McSweeney, and Sinha (1999) declare that:

> values greater than 0.75 or so may be taken to represent excellent agreement beyond chance, values below 0.40 or so may be taken to represent poor agreement beyond chance, and values between 0.40 and 0.75 may be taken to represent fair to good agreement beyond chance.
>
> (p. 6)

For percent agreement figures, Riffe, Lacy, and Fico (1998) state that, in communication research, 'a minimum level of 80% is usually the standard' (p. 128). Beyond the statistical context, content analysts suggest that researchers must decide for themselves the level of acceptable agreement. Riffe, Lacy, and Fico add the following: 'Research that is breaking new ground with concepts that are rich in analytical value may go ahead with reliability levels somewhat below that range' (p. 131). This lenience is based on the premise that some measures that are taken to increase reliability may simultaneously reduce the value of the results, or in Krippendorf's words 'reliability often gets in the way of validity' (1980, p. 130). Garrison, Anderson, and Archer (2000b), Hillman (1999), and McDonald (1998) reported kappas of 0.74, 0.96, and 0.67 respectively; however, it is premature to declare a conventional level of acceptability. We feel that the mere act of reporting these figures gives readers sufficient information to interpret results.

The difficulty of achieving acceptable levels of interrater reliability has led to the development of an alternative system of coding transcripts. Barros and Verdejo (2000), Duffy, Dueber, and Hawley (1998), and Ravenscroft and Pilkington (2000) have developed semi-structured computer conferencing systems, in which participants chose the type of contribution that they are making from a limited set of alternatives. For example, in the issue-based discussion forum of Duffy, Dueber, and Hawley's system, students post a message by selecting one of four labels – Hypothesis, Important Point, Evidence, or Learning Issue. To the content analyst, this means that students are essentially coding their own messages. Barros and Verdejo have developed a parallel system that also includes automatic message analysis features.

Replicability

The reliability of a coding scheme can be viewed as a continuum, beginning with coder stability (one coder agreeing with herself over time), to interrater reliability (two or more coders agreeing with each other), and ultimately to replicability (the ability of multiple and distinct groups of researchers to apply a coding scheme reliably). Thus, the definitive test of a coding scheme is replicability. The coding scheme that has been the basis for most attempts at replication originates in Henri's (1991) seminal article. However, each time her protocol is used, it is criticized and either modified or abandoned (Bullen, 1998; Gunawardena, Lowe, and Anderson, 1997; Hara, Bonk, and Angeli, 2000; Howell-Richardson and Mellar, 1996; Kanuka and Anderson, 1998; Newman, Webb, and Cochrane, 1995). The fact that Henri's procedure has drawn criticism is, paradoxically, complimentary since most researchers explicitly build upon the ideas enunciated by Henri – only her ideas have been criticized. No other model has generated attempts at replication; therefore, no other model has drawn significant criticism. This lack of replication (i.e., of successful applications of other researchers' coding schemes) should be regarded as a serious problem. In most fields, even when a valid study yields statistically significant findings, the results are described cautiously as 'supportive' until they have been replicated. Reliable application of a coding scheme by researchers who are not involved in its creation would be a convincing testament to its efficacy. Newman, Webb, and Cochrane (1995) conclude their study with an invitation to other researchers to apply and improve upon their protocol; likewise, Howell-Richardson and Mellar (1996) suggest that the validity of their method '. . . is an empirical question' (p. 53). With these statements, they are inviting others to test their method in practice. Unfortunately, to our knowledge no one has done so.

Systematic

In the context of content analysis, the term *systematic* refers to 'a more or less well structured set of ideas, assumptions, concepts and interpretative tendencies, which serves to structure the data of an area' (Reber, 1995, p. 780). Barros and Verdejo (2000) and Kanuka and Anderson's (1998) studies provide good models of systematic studies. At the outset of their investigation, Kanuka and Anderson recognized an association between the attributes of computer conferencing and the tenets of constructivism. Therefore, they began by identifying their perspective as constructivist and then selected a transcript analysis instrument that views communicative behavior in terms of active, collaborative, construction of knowledge. Other studies, however, combine irreconcilable paradigms in their analysis of data. Howell-Richardson and Mellar (1996) identify this issue in Henri's (1991) classification schema, noting that 'the level of description at the social, cognitive skills or interactivity levels was dependent on a mixture of theoretical approaches, which were not necessarily mutually consistent' (p. 69). As late as 1998, Bullen was casting a wide net, alternately sampling from Ennis' (1987) cognitive perspective of critical thinking, Henri's (1991) behaviorist perspective of interactivity, and Harasim's (1990) constructivist perspective of participation. The exploratory nature of these studies reflects the immaturity of the field rather than the deficiencies of the methodology or the nescience of the researchers. As in any new field of research, many of the studies in the sample were descriptive, with only a few experimental efforts. Both of these designs are described in the next section.

RESEARCH DESIGN

Descriptive

Berelson (1952) characterizes content analysis as primarily a descriptive technique. Of the 19 studies we reviewed, 18 were either partially or entirely descriptive – i.e., they described, organized and summarized what was occurring in a specific computer conference (see Table B.1). In these studies, information has been collected on several important themes associated with educational uses of computer conferencing, which gives subsequent researchers a foundation upon which they can build. For example, Bullen (1998) characterized participation in his group as 'low to medium' relative to participation levels in Harasim's (1990) study. These studies provide a rich source of anecdotal data and a model for the acquisition of fundamental information.

Experimental

Often researchers want to extend the purpose of content analysis from simple description to inferential hypothesis testing. Borg and Gall (1989) discuss this shift in the context of educational research: 'Whereas most early studies employing content analysis relied on simple frequency counts of objective variables (e.g., spelling errors), recent studies more often aim at using content analysis to gain insights into complex social and psychological variables' (p. 521). To this, they add the following caveat: 'Such studies are much more difficult to carry out than the simple frequency studies and often depend on a researcher's high level of sophistication' (p. 521).

Ahern, Peck, and Laycock's study of 1992 was the first in this domain to combine the content analysis technique with random assignment to groups and controlled manipulation of variables. This approach was advanced by Craig, Gholson, Ventura, and Graesser (2000), Howell-Richardson and Mellar (1996), and Marttunen (1997, 1998) who were able to draw convincing conclusions concerning different experimental or quasi-experimental conditions.

Our discussion now turns to the selection of the object of investigation. There is much to be learned from the study of both the manifest of latent content of transcripts; however, each of these types of content presents measurement challenges.

NATURE OF CONTENT

Manifest content

Manifest content is content that resides on the surface of communication and is therefore easily observable. An example of analyzing manifest content is provided by Rourke *et al.* (in press) who counted the number of times students addressed each other by name. The coding of manifest content can (at least in theory) be sufficiently formalized so as to be undertaken by machines, and imposes little interpretive burden upon coders (Hagelin, 1999). This ease of coding makes it attractive for content analysis. Berelson (1952), Holsti (1969), and Riffe, Lacy, and Fico (1998) concur that 'the requirements of scientific objectivity dictate that coding be restricted to manifest content' (Holsti, p. 12). Several important conferencing issues have been studied in this manner including participation, interaction, use of emoticons, and linguistic variation (see Table B.1). Doubtless, there are other manifest behaviors of interest to scholars of computer conferencing interactions that will be measured and described in future studies.

Latent content

Not all research questions, and especially not many of the most interesting ones, can be answered by focusing on the manifest or surface content of the transcripts. The overriding concern of many educational researchers is whether or not computer conferencing can facilitate higher-order learning outcomes, which educational theorists are coming to regard not as overt products, but rather as covert processes (Anderson and Garrison, 1995).

As early as 1951, Bales struggled with the problems of measuring latent behavior. In his study of face-to-face groups, Bales used two coders with a third operating an audio recorder for reliability checking. Coders using his system had to code in real time and were less able to, and less interested in, the analysis of long passages or sequential series of interactions. As Bales notes 'in a sense, the coder must work more or less on the surface meaning of activity, and forgo involved in-depth interpretations' (p. 35). Nonetheless, Bales rejected mechanistic counting of manifest variables in interaction analysis. He sought an interpretive analysis of behavior that 'involves the imputation of meaning, "the reading in" of content, the inference that the behavior has function(s) either by intent or effect' (p. 6). Like Bales, many educational researchers, including ourselves, are more interested in struggling with the important (though hidden) facets of individual and social cognition rather than assessing that which is most easily measured. Fortunately the temporal constraints and the necessity of staying attuned to non-verbal interaction that coders struggled with using Bale's system have been eliminated in the analysis of CMC transcripts.

Potter and Levine-Donnerstein (1999) make a further distinction between two types of latent content. The first they call *latent pattern* variables. As an example, they offer 'style of dress: formal or casual.' In making this type of coding decision, coders resort to an inventory of clues (e.g., ties, jewelry, etc.) that indicate the possible existence of the target variable; however, this possibility is confirmed only when other elements or an appropriate pattern of elements is concurrently present. An example of latent pattern variable analysis is provided by Marttunen (1997, 1998), who studied argumentation and counter-argumentation in students' email messages. Arguments were conceptualized as having four properties–claims, grounds, warrant, and rebuttals. The presence of one of these characteristics served to sensitize coders to the possibility that the message could be coded as an argument; however, judgement was withheld until more of the four properties, in an appropriate pattern, were identified.

Coding schemes for latent pattern variables are similar to, but more sophisticated than coding schemes for manifest variables. Interrater reliability increases as the list of indicators and cues approaches completeness, and coders are alert and well trained.

The same principles do not apply to *latent projective* variables. In latent projective variables, the locus of the variable shifts to the coder's interpretations of the meaning of the content. This is in contrast to both manifest and latent pattern variables, in which the meaning of the communication, or the target variable, resides on the surface of the content. Rourke *et al.* (in press) included the category 'use of humor' in their coding scheme and found that reliable coding depended on the intersubjectivity of coders' social and cognitive schemata. In other words, coders from different cultural backgrounds, ages, and personality types seem to have difficulty in reliably identifying humor and other latent projective variables.

In the studies that we reviewed, cognitive processes were the most commonly investigated latent variable. Henri's (1991) and Zhu's (1996) classification schemata look for 'cognitive' dimensions' in the transcripts. Others, beginning with Mason (1991), look for evidence of 'critical thinking' as it is variously defined (Bullen, 1998; Fahy *et al.*, 2000; Garrison, Anderson, and Archer, 2000b; and Newman, Johnson, Webb, and Cochrane, 1997).

Experienced content analysts argue that measuring latent content is inherently subjective and interpretative. Henri's taxonomy has been criticized on these grounds by Hara, Bonk, and Angeli (1998), Howell-Richardson and Mellar (1996), and Newman, Webb, and Cochrane (1995). Newman, Webb, and Cochrane's coding protocol that accompanies their instrument illustrates clearly the practical problems of identifying latent variables:

Rather than classify every statement in a transcript as, e.g., critical assessment or uncritical acceptance, we mark and count the obvious examples, and ignore the intermediate shades of grey. This eases the task of the assessors, since there is less need for subtle, subjective, borderline judgements . . . Of course, one statement might show more than one indicator, . . . Or indicators can even overlap.

(1995, p. 69)

The implications of this protocol on objectivity and reliability are obvious.

Instead of identifying latent variables during coding, Holsti (1969) suggests postponing this type of analysis to the interpretive stage, 'at which time,' he adds, 'the investigator is free to use all of his powers of imagination and intuition to draw meaningful conclusions from the data' (pp. 12–13). Two studies have taken this approach. To begin her study, Mason (1991) induced a typology of common communicative behaviors in conferencing transcripts. Her typology included six items such as 'use of personal experiences related to course themes, and reference to appropriate material outside the course package' (p. 168). Mason (1991) and Weiss and Morrison (1998) used these manifest elements to code the transcripts. Then, in the final stages of their studies, they proposed an association between the manifest behaviors and latent variables such as critical thinking, judgement, and initiative.

A more popular alternative has been to define the latent variables and then deduce manifest indicators of these variables (Bullen, 1998; Garrison, Anderson, and Archer, 2000b; Gunawardena, Lowe, and Anderson, 1997; Henri, 1991; Marttunen, 1997; McDonald, 1998; Newman, Webb, and Cochrane, 1995; Zhu, 1996; Rourke *et al.*, in press). For example, Henri's 'surface processing' category was identified in the transcript through indicators such as 'repeating what has been said without adding any new elements' (p. 130). Both of these approaches, inductive and deductive, have been useful for studying latent variables through a survey of manifest content. Identifying the target variables as manifest or latent will influence the determination of the unit of analysis, a process that is discussed in the next section.

UNIT OF ANALYSIS

Part of conducting a quantitative study involves identifying the segments of the transcript that will be recorded and categorized. In content analysis nomenclature, this process is called *unitizing*. Researchers have experimented with different types of recording units with varying degrees of success. Their goal has been to select a unit that multiple coders can identify reliably, and simultaneously, one that exhaustively and exclusively encompasses the sought-after construct. The research that we reviewed in this article points to a frustrating negative correlation between these two criteria. Fixed units such as single words or entire messages are objectively recognizable, but they do not always properly encompass the construct under investigation.

Dynamic units such as Henri's (1991) 'unit of meaning' properly delimit the construct, but invite subjective and inconsistent identification of the unit.

Sentence unit

Units such as the word, proposition, or the sentence are called *syntactical units* because they are delimited by syntactical criteria. Fahy *et al.* (2000) and Hillman (1999) used the sentence as their recording unit to help meet the goal of developing instruments that are easy to use and reliable. During a preliminary analysis, Fahy *et al.* reported percent agreement figures as high as 94% and Hillman reported a kappa of 0.96 for the three variables investigated in his study. Our experience with this unit of analysis was less encouraging. The objectivity of a syntactical unit is confounded by the idiosyncratic nature of conferencing communications (Blanchette, 1999). The syntax in the conferences we studied combined the telegraphic style of email with the informality of oral conversation. The following selection from one of our transcripts is typical:

> Certain subjects could be called training subjects . . . i.e., How to apply artificial respiration . . . .as in first aid . . . and though you may want to be a guide on the side . . . one must know the correct procedures in order to teach competency . . . other subjects lead themselves very well to exploration and comment/research [ellipses in original].

How many sentences are present in the preceding transcript selection? The strength of the sentence unit – reliable identification – did not materialize in this example. Use of the sentence unit also introduces an additional subjective step to the research process in that coders must first interpret the messages posted by the participants in the conference and transform them into sentences. Also, sentence level coding yields an enormous number of cases. Hillman reports an average of 8680 sentences in each of the transcripts he analyzed.

Paragraph unit

Hara, Bonk, and Angeli (2000) attempted to use a slightly larger syntactical unit, the paragraph. Use of this unit could significantly reduce the number of cases, as compared to the number generated by the use of the sentence unit. However, as the size of the unit expands, so does the likelihood that the unit will encompass multiple variables. Conversely, one variable may span multiple paragraphs. Also, our experience did not support the authors' optimistic statement that 'college-level students should be able to break down the messages into paragraphs' (p. 9). Often, a full line of space or a tab was used for purposes other than delimiting a single coherent and unified idea accompanied by a group of supporting sentences. And, once the syntactical criteria are lost, the definition of the unit as 'paragraph' becomes meaningless: What the coders are identifying are, in fact, graphical blocks of text. Hara, Bonk, and Angeli's (2000) ad hoc coding protocol reveals these problems: '. . . when two continuous paragraphs dealt with the same ideas, they were each counted as a separate unit. And when one paragraph contained two ideas, it was counted as a two separate units' (p. 9). Using this protocol, Hara, Bonk, and Angeli settled for an aggregate percent agreement figure of 74.6%, which was '. . . deemed adequate given the subjectiveness of such scoring criteria' (p. 9).

Message unit

Marttunen (1997, 1998) looked for levels of argumentation and counter-argumentation in transcripts, and like Ahern, Peck, and Laycock (1992) and Garrison, Anderson, and Archer (2000b) used the message as the unit of analysis. This unit has important advantages. First, it is objectively identifiable: Unlike other units of analysis, multiple raters can agree consistently on the total number of cases. Second, it produces a manageable set of cases. Marttunen, and Ahern, Peck, and Laycock recorded a total of 545 and 185 messages respectively, a total that would obviously have been considerably larger if the messages had been subdivided. Third, it exhaustively and exclusively contained the object of Marttunen's and Ahern, Peck, and Laycock's studies. Fourth, it is a unit whose parameters are determined by the author of the message. In the discussion of interrater reliability, Marttunen reported a reliability (r) of 0.71; Ahern, Peck, and Laycock reported percent agreement at 'over 90%' (p. 298), and Garrison, Anderson, and Archer reported a kappa of 0.74 when using the message unit as the unit of analysis.

Thematic unit

Unfortunately, the message is not suitable for all variables. The most commonly used unit in our sample was introduced by Henri (1991), who rejected the process of a priori and authoritatively fixing the size of the unit based on criteria that are tangential to the construct under study. Instead, she used a 'unit of meaning,' which is similar in form to the conventional *thematic unit* described by Budd, Thorp, and Donohue (1967) as '. . . a single thought unit or idea unit that conveys a single item of information extracted from a segment of content' (p. 34). Henri justifies this approach by arguing that 'it is absolutely useless to wonder if it is the word, the proposition, the sentence or the paragraph which is the proper unit of meaning, for the unit of meaning is lodged in meaning' (p. 134). However, coding a complex, latent construct such as 'in-depth processing' with a volatile unit such as the 'meaning unit' creates extensive opportunity for subjective ratings and low reliability. Not surprisingly, Henri offers no reliability discussion.

Illocutionary unit

Howell-Richardson and Mellar (1996) attempted to improve the reliability of this procedure by establishing a theoretical basis for Henri's meaning unit. Drawing on Speech-Act theory, Howell-Richardson and Mellar explained that transcripts should be viewed with the following question in mind: What is the purpose of a particular utterance? A change in purpose sets the parameters for the unit. The authors evaded some of the difficulties that Henri's scheme presents by focusing on manifest content such as the linguistic properties of a message and the audience to whom it was directed. Howell-Richardson and Mellar's method has advantages; however, rather than reporting interrater reliability figures, the authors submit the following tantalizing discussion:

> Our procedure overcomes both the problem of relying on potentially inconsistent judgements in deciding whether or not a set of wordings constitute a single meaning or more than one and the problem of suggesting that graphic boundaries of the message can be equated with a single communicative act.
>
> (1996, p. 52)

The selection of the unit of analysis is complex and challenging for the quantitative content analysis researcher. Krippendorf (1980) concedes that, ultimately, the process of unitization 'involves considerable compromise' (p. 64) between meaningfulness, productivity, efficiency, and reliability.

SOFTWARE TO AID CONTENT ANALYSIS

The existence of machine-readable data (the conference transcripts) does not guarantee that the transcripts are available in a format that can easily be analyzed. A first problem is gathering the data into a single text file that contains the entire sampling unit. Some conferencing software does not support export of the complete conference or selected portions, but rather forces researchers to tediously cut and paste each individual message from a separate window into a larger text file.

Once the data have been moved into a text file, there are a number of software packages that can be used to assist in the process of analysis. The most useful are qualitative analysis packages such as Atlas/ti®, NUD*IST® and HyperQual®. These packages allow the researcher to identify the unit of analysis in the transcript and assign the text to a coding category that has been theoretically defined apriori or to one that emerges from the analysis process. Later analysis can combine or sort codes into families for more meaningful discussion, presentation or analysis. These packages allow multiple coding of individual passages for use when more than one construct is being investigated and also allow multiple coders to work on a single coding task while maintaining identification of the coder for calculation of reliability. A wide variety of reports can be generated from these packages including list and frequency counts of codes with or without illustrative quotations from the text.

In addition to the hand coding by researchers, many of these packages allow coding to be automated, based upon multistring text search and pattern matching. Other quantitative data can be generated, including number of sentences, coding results by individual posters, and counts of results from multiple documents.

Once the content of the transcripts had been coded and categorized, SPSS or other statistical programs can be employed for more quantitative analyses and calculation of reliability. Percent agreement calculations are performed using SPSS's chi square function, and final interrater reliability figures can be calculated with SPSS's Cohen's kappa statistic.

ETHICS

We conclude with a brief discussion of the ethical issues related to content analysis of computer conferencing transcripts. Questions of ethical approval and informed consent are important to all researchers and their subjects. We have had personal experience in which a proposed study was funded and then aborted due to the reluctance of a single individual to allow external researchers to review the contents of the computer conference transcript. Alternatively, we have been involved in the tedious process of obtaining ethical clearance from a university ethics approval board and have been left wondering if the approval was either useful or necessary.

Our experience as researchers in a Canadian university operating under ethical approval guidelines set by our university and required by Canadian federal research granting councils is probably similar to that of researchers operating under other jurisdictions. However, each research team should investigate policies and practices that apply in their particular circumstances.

Ethical guidelines have been established to protect human subjects from harm as a result of participation in scientific investigation. The three Canadian federal granting councils released a Code of Ethical Conduct for Research Involving Humans in 1994 (http://www.mrc.gc.ca/ethics/code/english/toc.html). This Code cites four principles to guide researchers in construction and evaluation of research protocols. These principles are 1) respect for persons, 2) non-maleficence, 3) beneficence, and 4) justice.

The respect for persons principle is grounded upon the right of participants to make informed choice as to degree (if any) of participation in the study. This is the area of greatest issue to many researchers. This code defines research participants as 'living individuals or groups of living individuals about whom a scholar conducting research obtains (1) data through intervention or interaction with the individual or group, or (2) identifiable private information.' Distinguishing between active action research in which the researcher takes part in the conference under investigation and research projects in which the researcher merely examines the subsequent transcript, changes the nature of the 'intervention or interaction' between researcher and research subject. We argue that researchers analyzing the transcripts of a conference, without participating in the conference, have not intervened in the process and thus have not placed themselves in the position of research participants. However, the second criterion is relevant in that often transcripts contain 'private information' that has been posted to the conferencing group.

Two solutions to this problem are possible. The researcher can request that each participant sign a conventional informed consent release form in which the standard information is provided to participants describing: nature of the investigation, potential harm and benefits, how the information obtained is to be used, and how the participants can contact the researchers to discuss any concerns they may have. This standard process of subject permission is complicated in a formal education context in which protection of privacy may preclude the release of addresses of students to which the researcher can post release forms. In our experience, transmitting such forms by email or posting messages within an administration section of the computer conference results in the majority of students responding positively to the request, none objecting, but a few not replying at all. In the worst case, a negative response, or lack of any response, forces researchers to either abandon this sample group or have the postings of individuals who have not given permission removed from the transcript prior to analysis. Removal of individual postings is possible using search and delete techniques of the analysis software, but in practice becomes problematic in that postings often contain excerpts and quotations from previous postings, any of which may have been made by non-participating subjects. In addition, use of personal names is common and eradicating all references to non-participants can be very time consuming. Further, one could narrowly define removal of a non-participant's posting itself as an analysis process requiring permission of the participants. Finally, the removal of one or more person's postings may make understanding of the conference text impossible and decontextualize subsequent postings.

A second more encompassing solution is to reduce the requirement for informed consent by applying the two criteria of the 'research participant' above and concluding that transcript analysis participants are not, by definition research participants. To arrive at such a conclusion one must address the second stipulation that the researcher not obtain 'identifiable private information.' The use of 'search and replace' features of analysis software is then used to change all personal or login names from headers of postings and within the postings to 'subject 1, subject 2', etc.

The study of computer conferencing transcripts seems to present little danger of maleficence, and we believe high potential for beneficence – especially in potential to increase learning efficacy of subsequent conferences. The issue of justice seems not to be of major concern and is normally an issue only when conducting research with specialized target groups based on gender, race or social economic status. Thus the issue of informed consent seems to be the most problematic ethics issue for transcript analysis researchers. There seems to be no easy solution to this problem, other than for researchers to expect to expend some considerable energy obtaining consent or stripping non-participant postings or personal identification from the transcripts.

CONCLUSION

In 1996, Mason and Romiszowski remarked that:

> The most glaring omission in CMC research continues to be the lack of analytical techniques applied to the content of the conference transcript. Given that the educational value of computer conferencing is much touted by enthusiasts, it is remarkable that so few evaluators are willing to tackle this research area.
>
> (Mason and Romiszowski, 1996, p. 443)

As conferencing matures and diffuses, naïve enthusiasm is giving way to practical questions about how this technology can be used to facilitate specific educational objectives. This attitude is leading to a shift in the literature away from anecdotal, promotional essays towards more objective research. We hope that a portion of this research will exploit the quantitative content analysis technique.

The 19 studies that we surveyed have demonstrated the value of this research technique for both descriptive and experimental purposes. The authors of these studies have also addressed many of the methodological problems that hinder the application of this technique to educational computer conferencing transcripts.

The main shortcoming of the quantitative content analysis studies in our sample was the failure of researchers to adhere to the principles that make quantitative research valid. Characteristics such as objectivity and reliability are not accidental features of some studies; rather, they are important criteria for any studies using this technique. As Riffe, Lacy, and Fico (1998) insist, 'failure to report reliability virtually invalidates whatever usefulness a content study may have' (p. 134).

In our own studies we are examining the use of computer conferencing to support higher order learning through peer and instructor interaction. (Garrison, Anderson, and Archer, 2000a; Garrison, Anderson, and Archer, 2000b; Rourke *et al.*, in press). We are attempting to develop transcript analysis tools that are efficient, reliable, valid, and practical so that they may be used to evaluate conference activity not only by researchers, but also by teachers and instructional designers. The task of developing instruments and techniques for transcript analysis that meet these criteria is a necessary prerequisite to the empirical investigation of asynchronous, text-based computer conferencing. Further studies are needed to identify the salient elements of this medium. Not all of the original hyperbolic claims for the benefits of computer conferencing have been empirically tested. Does asynchronous communication really foster more reflective and careful response composition? Does text-based communication actually lead to more articulate presentation of arguments? If these claims are supported, then experimental designs will play an important role in defining exactly how to facilitate this potential. To answer these increasingly important questions being asked about the use of computer conferencing in higher education, we need to undertake rigorous and systematic research studies.

ACKNOWLEDGEMENTS

This study is supported in part by a grant from the Social Sciences and Humanities Research Council of Canada.

REFERENCES

Ahern, T., Peck, K., and Laycock, M. (1992). The effects of teacher discourse in computer-mediated discussion. *Journal of Educational Computing Research*, 8, 3, 291–309.

Anderson, T. and Garrison, D. R. (1995). Critical thinking in distance education: Developing critical communities in an audio teleconference context. *Higher Education*, 29, 183–199.

Anderson, T. and Kanuka, H. (1997). On-line forums: New platforms for professional development and group collaboration. (ERIC Document Reproduction Service, ED 418 693).

Bales, R. (1951). *Interaction process analysis*. Cambridge: Addison-Wesley.

Barros, B. and Verdejo, F. (2000). Analyzing student interaction processes in order to improve collaboration: The DEGREE approach. *International Journal of Artificial Intelligence in Education*, 11, to appear.

Bereiter, C., and Scardemalia, M. (1987). *The psychology of written composition*. Hillsdale NJ: Lawrence Erlbaum Associates.

Berelson, B. (1952). *Content analysis in communication research*. Illinois: Free Press.

Blanchette, J. (1999). Register choice: Linguistic variation in an online classroom. *International Journal of Educational Telecommunications*, 5, 2, 127–142.

Borg, W. and Gall, M. (1989). The methods and tools of observational research. In W. Borg and M. Gall (Eds.) *Educational research: An introduction* (5th ed.), pp. 473–530. London: Longman.

Budd, R., Thorp, R., and Donohue, L. (1967). *Content analysis of communications*. London: The Collier-McMillan Limited.

Bullen, M. (1998). Participation and critical thinking in online university distance education. *Journal of Distance Education*, 13. 2, 1–32.

Capozzoli, M., McSweeney, L., and Sinha, D. (1999). Beyond kappa: A review of interrater agreement measures. *The Canadian Journal of Statistics*, 27, 1, 3–23.

Cohen. J. (1960). A coefficient of agreement for nominal scales. *Educational and Psychological Measurement*, 20, 37–46.

Craig, S., Gholson, B., Ventura, M., Graesser, A., and The Tutoring Research Group (2000). Overhearing dialogues and monologues in virtual tutoring sessions: Effects on questioning and vicarious learning. *International Journal of Artificial Intelligence in Education*, 11, to appear.

Duffy, T., Dueber, B., and Hawley, C. (1998). Critical thinking in a distributed environment: A pedagogical base for the design of conferencing systems. In C. Bonk and K. King (Eds.) *Electronic collaborators: Learner-centered technologies for literacy, apprenticeship, and discourse*, pp. 51–78. New Jersey: Lawrence Erlbaum Associates, Publishers.

Ennis, R. (1987). A taxonomy of critical thinking dispositions and abilities. In J. B. Baron and R. J. Sternberg (Eds.) *Teaching thinking skills: Theory and practice*, pp. 9–26. New York: Freeman.

Fahy, P. J., Crawford, G., Ally, M., Cookson, P., Keller, V., and Prosser, F. (2000). The development and testing of a tool for analysis of computer mediated conferencing transcripts. *Alberta Journal of Educational Research*, 46, 1, Spring, 85–88.

Flanders, N. (1970). *Analyzing teacher behavior*. Reading, MA: Addison-Wesley.

Garrison, D. R., Anderson, T., and Archer, W. (2000a). Critical thinking in a text-based environment. Computer conferencing in higher education. *Internet in Higher Education*, 2, 2, 87–105.

Garrison, D. R., Anderson, T., and Archer, W. (2000b). Critical thinking and computer conferencing: A model and tool to assess cognitive presence. Submitted for publication

Gunawardena, C., Lowe, C., and Anderson, T. (1997). Analysis of a global on-line debate and the development of an interaction analysis model for examining social construction of knowledge in computer conferencing. *Journal of Educational Computing Research*, 17, 4, 395–429.

Hagelin, E. (1999). Coding data from child health records: The relationship between interrater agreement and interpretive burden. *Journal of Pediatric Nursing*, 14, 5, 313–321.

Hara, N., Bonk, C., and Angeli, C., (2000). Content analyses of on-line discussion in an applied educational psychology course. *Instructional Science*, 28, 2, 115–152.

Harasim, L. (1990). *On-line education: Perspectives on a new environment*. New York: Praeger.

Henri, F. (1991). Computer conferencing and content analysis. In A. Kaye (Ed.) *Collaborative learning through computer conferencing: The Najaden papers*, (pp. 117–136). London: Springer-Verlag.

Hillman, D. (1999). A new method for analysing patterns of interaction. *The American Journal of Distance Education*, 13, 2, 37–47.

Holsti, O. (1969). *Content analysis for the social sciences and humanities*. Don Mills: Addison-Wesley Publishing Company.

Howell-Richardson, C. and Mellar, H. (1996). A methodology for the analysis of patterns of participation within computer mediated communication courses. *Instructional Science*, 24, 47–69.

Kanuka, H. and Anderson, T. (1998). Online social interchange, discord, and knowledge construction. *Journal of Distance Education*, 13, 1, 57–75.

Krippendorf, K. (1980). *Quantitative content analysis: An introduction to its method*. Beverly Hills: Sage Publications.

Marttunen, M. (1997). Electronic mail as a pedagogical delivery system. *Research in Higher Education*, 38, 3, 345–363.

Marttunen, M. (1998). Learning of argumentation in face-to-face and e-mail environments. (ERIC Document Reproduction Service, ED 422 791).

Mason, R. (1991). Analyzing computer conferencing interactions. *Computers in Adult Education and Training*, 2, 3, 161–173.

Mason, R. and Romiszowski, A. (1996). Computer-mediated communication. In D. Jonassen (Ed.). *Handbook of Research for Educational Communications and Technology*. New York: Macmillan.

McDonald, J. (1998). Interpersonal group dynamics and development in computer conferencing: The rest of the story. In *Wisconsin Distance Education Proceedings* Tri-Council Policy Statement: Ethical Conduct for Research Involving Humans. Available [Online]: http://www.mrc.gc.ca/publications/publications.html.

Mower, D. (1996). A content analysis of student/instructor communication via computer conferencing. *Higher Education*, 32, 217–241.

Newman, G., Johnson, C., Webb, B., and Cochrane, C. (1997). Evaluating the quality of learning in computer supported co-operative learning. *Journal of the American Society for Information Science*, 48, 6, 484–495.

Newman, G., Webb, B., and Cochrane, C. (1995). A content analysis method to measure critical thinking in face-to-face and computer supported group learning. *Interpersonal Computing and Technology*, 3, 2, 56–77. Available [Online]: http://www.helsinki.fi/science/optek/1995/n2/newman.txt.

Potter, W. and Levine-Donnerstein, D. (1999). Rethinking validity and reliability in content analysis. *Journal of Applied Communication Research*, 27, 258–284.

Ravenscroft, A. and Pilkington, R. (2000). Investigation by design: Developing dialogue models to support reasoning and conceptual change. *International Journal of Artificial Intelligence in Education*, 11, to appear.

Reber, A. (1995). *Dictionary of psychology* (2nd ed.). Toronto: Penguin Books.

Riffe, D., Lacy, S., and Fico, F. (1998). *Analyzing media messages: Quantitative content analysis*. New Jersey: Lawrence Erlbaum Associates, Inc.

Rourke, L., Anderson, T., Archer, W., and Garrison, R. (in press). Assessing social presence in computer conferencing transcripts. *Canadian Journal of Distance Education*.

Sinclair, J., and Coulthard, M. (1975). *Towards an analysis of discourse.* London: Oxford University Press.

Weiss, R. and Morrison, G. (1998). Evaluation of a graduate seminar conducted by listserv. (ERIC Document Reproduction Service, ED 423 868).

Zhu, E. (1996). Meaning negotiation, knowledge construction, and mentoring in a distance learning course. (ERIC Document Reproduction Service, ED 397 849).

References

Achenbach, J. (1999) 'The too-much-information age', *The Washington Post*, March 12, A23.

Advisory Committee for Online Learning (2000) *The e-learning e-volution in colleges and universities: A pan-Canadian challenge*, Ottawa: Industry Canada.

Anderson, T. (2001) 'The hidden curriculum of distance education', *Change Magazine*, 33, 6: 29–35.

Anderson, T. D. and Garrison, D. R. (1997) 'New roles for learners at a distance', in C. C. Gibson (ed.), *Distance learners in higher education: Institutional responses for quality outcomes*, Madison, WI: Atwood Publishing.

Anderson, T. and Mason, R. (1993) 'The Bangkok Project: New tool for professional development', *American Journal of Distance Education*, 7, 2: 5–18.

Anderson, T., Rourke, L., Garrison, D. R. and Archer, W. (2001) 'Assessing teacher presence in a computer conferencing context', *Journal of Asynchronous Learning Networks*, 5, 2. Available [Online]: http://www.aln.org/alnweb/journal/Vol5_issue2/Anderson/5-2%20JALN%20Anderson%20Assessing.htm. Retrieved 6 June 2002.

Anderson, T., Varnhagen, S. and Campbell, K. (1998) 'Faculty adoption of teaching and learning technologies: Contrasting earlier adopters and mainstream faculty', *Canadian Journal of Higher Education*, 28, 3: 71–98. Available [Online]: http://www.aln.org/alnweb/journal/jaln-vol5issue2v2.htm.

Archer, W., Garrison, D. R. and Anderson, T. (1999) 'Adopting disruptive technologies in traditional universities: Continuing education as an incubator for innovation', *Canadian Journal of University Continuing Education*, 25, 1: 13–30.

Bates, T. (1995) *Technology, open learning and distance education*, London: Routledge.

Bereiter, C. (1992) 'Referent-centred and problem-centred knowledge: Elements of an educational epistemology', *Interchange*, 23, 337–361.

Bereiter, C. and Scardemalia, M. (1987) *The psychology of written composition*, Hillsdale NJ: Lawrence Erlbaum Associates.

Berners-Lee, T. (1999) *Weaving the Web: The original design and ultimate destiny of the World Wide Web by its inventor*, San Francisco: Harper.

Berners-Lee, T., Hendler, J. and Lassila, O. (2001) 'The semantic web', *Scientific American*, May.

Biggs, J. B. (1987) *Student approaches to learning and studying*, Melbourne, Australia: Australian Council for Educational Research.

Blanchette, J. (2001) 'Questions in the online learning environment', *Journal of Distance Education*, 16, 2: 37–57.

Bonk, C. J. and Dennen, N. (in press) 'Framework for frameworks in Web instruction: Fostering research, design, benchmarks, training, and pedagogy', in M. G. Moore and B. Anderson (eds) *Handbook of American distance education*, Mahwah, NJ: Lawrence Erlbaum.

Brookfield, S. D. (1987) 'Recognizing critical thinking', in S. D. Brookfield (ed.) *Developing Critical Thinkers*, Oxford: Jossey-Bass Publishers.

Brookfield, S. D. (1990) *The skillful teacher*, San Francisco: Jossey-Bass.

Brown, J. S. (2000) 'Growing up digital: How the Web changes work, education, and the ways people learn', *Change*, March/April, 11–20.

Brown, J. S. and Duguid, P. (1996) 'Universities in the digital age', *Change*, July/August, 11–19.

Campion, M. and Renner, W. (1992) 'The supposed demise of Fordism: Implications for distance education and higher education', *Distance Education*, 13, 1: 7–28.

Cecez-Kecmanovic, D. and Webb, C. (2000) 'Towards a communicative model of collaborative web-mediated learning', *Australian Journal of Educational Technology*, 16, 1:73–85.

Chandler, D. (1995) *The act of writing: A media theory approach*, Aberystwyth: University of Wales.

Christensen, C. (1997) *The innovator's dilemma: when new technologies cause great firms to fail*, Boston: Harvard Business School Press.

Clark, B. R. (1998). *Creating entrepreneurial universities: Organizational pathways of transformation*, Guildford: Pergamon.

Clark, R. E. (1983) 'Reconsidering research on learning from media', *Review of Educational Research*, 53: 445–459.

Clark, R. (1994) 'Media will never influence learning', *Educational Technology Research and Development*, 42, 3: 21–29.

Clark, R. (2000) 'Evaluating distance education: strategies and cautions, *Quarterly Review of Distance Education*, 1, 1: 3–16.

Coleman, S. D., Perry, J. D. and Schwen, T. M. (1997) 'Constructivist instructional development: Reflecting on practice from an alternative paradigm', in C. Dills and A. Romiszowski (eds) *Instructional development paradigms*, Englewood Cliffs, NJ: Educational Technology Publications, pp. 269–282.

Collison, G., Elbaum, B., Haavind, S. and Tinker, R. (2000) *Facilitating online learning: Effective strategies for moderators*, Madison, WI: Atwood Publishing.

Curtin University (2001) *Internet based learning construction kit*. Available [Online]: http://www.curtin.edu.au/home/allen/we3/igm/12050108.html.

Davie, L. (1989) 'Facilitation techniques for the online tutor', in R. Mason and A. Kaye (eds) *MindWeave*, Oxford: Pergamon Press, pp. 74–85.

Dede, C. (1996) 'The evolution of distance education: Emerging technologies and distributed learning', *American Journal of Distance Education*, 10, 2: 4–36.

de la Sola Pool, I. (1984) *Communications flows: A consensus in the United States and Japan*, Amsterdam: University of Tokyo Press.

Dewey, J. (1916) *Democracy and education*, New York: Macmillan.

Dewey, J. (1933) *How we think* (rev. ed.), Boston, MA: D.C. Heath.

Dewey, J. (1938) *Experience and education*, New York: Collier Macmillan.

Dewey, J. (1967) 'Psychology', in J. A. Boydston (ed.) *John Dewey: The early works,*

1882–1898, Vol. 2, Carbondale, IL: Southern Illinois University Press, pp. 204–213. (Original work published 1887).

Dewey, J. and Childs, J. L. (1981) 'The underlying philosophy of education', in J. A. Boydston, (ed.) *John Dewey: The later works, 1925–1953, Vol. 8*, Carbondale, IL: Southern Illinois University Press, pp. 77–103. (Original work published 1933).

Dirks, M. (1997). *Developing an appropriate assessment strategy: Research and guidance for practice*, web.97 (ed.), Northern Arizona University.

Dolence, M. and Norris, D. (1995) *Transforming higher education: A vision for learning in the 21st century*, Ann Arbor, MI: Society for College and University Planning.

Donovan, M. S., Bransford, J. D. and Pellegrino, J. W. (1999) *How people learn: Bridging research and practice*, Washington, DC: National Academy Press.

Downes, S. (2000) 'Learning Objects', retrieved 21 May 2001, from the World Wide Web: http://www.atl.ualberta.ca/downes/naweb/column000523.htm. Available [Online]: http://www.downes.ca/files/Learning_Objects_whole.htm.

Eaton, J. S. (2001). *Distance learning: Academic and political challenges for higher education accreditation*, CHEA Monograph Series, No. 1, Council for Higher Education Accreditation.

Entwistle, N. J. and Ramsden, P. (1983) *Understanding student learning*, London: Croom Helm.

Fabro, K. R. and Garrison, D. R. (1998) 'Computer conferencing and higher-order learning', *Indian Journal of Open Learning*, 7, 1: 41–54.

Feenberg, A. (1999) *Questioning technology*, London: Routledge.

Frye, B. E. (2002) 'Reflections', *EDUCAUSE*, 37, 1: 8–14.

Garrison, D. R. (1985) 'Three generations of technological innovations in distance education', *Distance Education*, 6, 2: 235–241.

Garrison, D. R. (1997a) 'Computer conferencing: The post-industrial age of distance education', *Open Learning*, 12, 2: 3–11.

Garrison, D. R. (1997b) 'Self-directed learning: Toward a comprehensive model', *Adult Education Quarterly*, 48, 1: 18–33.

Garrison, D. R. (2001) 'Research based continuing studies: A transformational leadership model', *Canadian Journal of University Continuing Education*, 27, 1: 77–97.

Garrison, D. R. and Anderson, T. (1999) 'Avoiding the industrialization of research universities: Big and little distance education', *American Journal of Distance Education*, 13, 2: 48–63.

Garrison, D. R. and Anderson, T. (2000) 'Transforming and enhancing university teaching: Stronger and weaker technological influences', in T. Evans and D. Nation (eds), *Changing university teaching: Reflections on creating educational technologies*, London: Kogan Page.

Garrison, D. R., Anderson, T. and Archer, W. (2000) 'Critical inquiry in a text-based environment: Computer conferencing in higher education', *The Internet and Higher Education*, 2, 2/3: 87–105.

Garrison, D. R., Anderson, T. and Archer, W. (2001) 'Critical thinking, cognitive presence and computer conferencing in distance education', *American Journal of Distance Education*, 15, 1: 7–23.

Garrison, D. R. and Archer, W. (2000) *A transactional perspective on teaching and learning: A framework for adult and higher education*, Oxford, UK: Pergamon.

Garrison, D. R. and Baynton, M. (1987) 'Beyond independence in distance education: The concept of control', *American Journal of Distance Education*, 1, 3: 3–15.

Garrison, D. R. and Shale, D. (1990) 'A new framework and perspective', in D. R. Garrison and D. Shale (eds) *Education at a distance: From issues to practice*, Malabar, FL: Robert E. Krieger Publishing Company, pp. 123–133.

Garrison, J. (1997) *Dewey and eros: Wisdom and desire in the art of teaching*, New York: Teachers College Press.

Gilbert, S. W. (2000) 'So, why bother?', *AAHESGIT*, 49. Available [Online]: http://www.tltgroup.org/gilbert/WhyBother.htm. Retrieved 6 June 2002.

Gunawardena, C. N. (1991) 'Collaborative learning and group dynamics in computer-mediated communication networks', *Research Monograph of the American Center for the Study of Distance Education*, 9: 14–24, University Park, Pennsylvania: The Pennsylvania State University.

Gunawardena, C. N. (1995) 'Social presence theory and implications for interaction and collaborative learning in computer conferencing', Paper presented at the Fourth International Conference on Computer Assisted Instruction, Hsinchu, Taiwan.

Hannafin, M. J. (1989) 'Inter-action strategies and emerging instructional technologies: Psychological perspectives', *Canadian Journal of Educational Communication*, 18: 167–179.

Harasim, L. (1987) 'Teaching and learning on-line: Issues in computer-mediated graduate courses', *Canadian Journal of Educational Communication*, 16: 117–135.

Harasim, L. M. (1989) 'On-line education: A new domain', in R. Mason and A. R. Kaye (eds) *Mindweave: Communication, computers, and distance education*, New York: Pergamon, pp. 50–62.

Harasim, L., Hiltz, S. R., Teles, L. and Turoff, M. (1995) *Learning networks: A field guide to teaching and learning online*, Cambridge, MA: MIT Press.

Hiltz, S. R. and Turoff, M. (1993) *The network nation: Human communication via computer*, Cambridge, MA: MIT Press.

Holmberg, B. (1989) *Theory and practice of distance education*, London: Routledge.

Ikenberry, S. O. (1999) 'The university and the information age', in W. Z. Hirsch and L. E. Weber (eds) *Challenges facing higher education at the millennium*, Phoenix, AZ: Oryx Press.

Jiang, M. and Ting, E. (2000) 'A study of factors influencing students' perceived learning in a web-based course environment', *International Journal of Educational Telecommunications*, 6, 4: 317–338.

Kanuka, H. and Anderson, T. (1998) 'Online social interchange, discord, and knowledge construction', *Journal of Distance Education*, 13, 1: 57–75.

Kaufman, D. (1989) 'Third generation course design in distance education', in R. Sweet (ed.) *Post-secondary distance education in Canada*, Athabasca, AB: Canadian Society for Studies in Education, pp. 61–78.

Kaye, T. (1987) 'Introducing computer-mediated communication into a distance education system', *Canadian Journal of Educational Communication*, 16: 153–166.

Kozma, R. (1994) 'Will media influence learning? Reframing the debate', *Educational Technology Research & Development*, 42, 2: 7–19.

Langer, E. (1997) *The power of mindful learning*, Reading, MA: Addison-Wesley.

Laurillard, D. (1997) *Rethinking university teaching: A framework for the effective use of educational technology*, London: Routledge.

Laurillard, D. (2000) 'New technologies and the curriculum', in P. Scott (ed.) *Higher Education Re-formed*, London: Falmer Press, pp. 133–153.

Laurillard, D. (2002) 'Rethinking teaching for the knowledge society', *EDUCAUSE*, 37, 1: 16–25.

Lauzon, A. C. and Moore, G. A. B. (1989) 'A fourth generation distance education system: Integrating computer-assisted learning and computer conferencing', *The American Journal of Distance Education*, 3, 1: 38–49.

Lave, J. (1988) *Cognition in practice: Mind, mathematics, and culture in everyday life*, Cambridge: Cambridge University Press.

Lea, M. (2001) 'Computer conferencing and assessment: New ways of writing in higher education', *Studies in Higher Education*, 26, 2: 163–181.

Lipman, M. (1991) *Thinking in education*, Cambridge: Cambridge University Press.

Machiavelli, N. (1950) *The prince*, New York: Random House.

Marton, F. (1988) 'Describing and improving teaching', in R.R. Schmeck (ed.) *Learning strategies and learning styles*, New York: Plenum.

Marton, F. and Ramsden, P. (1988) 'What does it take to improve learning?', in P. Ramsden (ed.) *Improving learning: New perspectives*, London: Kogan Page.

Marton, F. and Saljo, R. (1976) 'On qualitative differences in learning: I – Outcome and process', *British Journal of Educational Psychology*, 46: 4–11.

McLuhan, M. (1995) *Understanding media: The extensions of man*, Cambridge, MA: The MIT Press.

Mehrabian, A. (1969) 'Some referents and measures of nonverbal behavior', *Behavior Research Methods and Instrumentation*, 1, 6: 205–207.

MIT (2000) *Software Agents Group*, Retrieved 21 May 2001. Available [Online]: http://mevard.www.media.mit.edu/groups/agents/.

Moore, D. (2000) 'The changing face of the infosphere', *Internet Computing*, 4, 1: Retrieved 6 June 2002. Available (Online): http://www.computer.org/internet/v4n1/moore.htm

Moore, G. (1991) *Crossing the chasm*, New York: Harper Business.

Moore, M. and Kearsley, G. (1996) *Distance education: A systems view*, Toronto: Wadsworth Publishing Company.

Murray, J. H. (1997) *Hamlet on the holodeck: The future of narrative in cyberspace*, New York: Free Press.

Myers, K. (1999) 'Is there a place for instructional design in the information age?', *Educational Technology*, 36, 6: 50–53.

Nipper, S. (1989) 'Third generation distance learning and computer conferencing', in R. Mason and A. A. Kaye (eds) *Mindweave: Communication, computers and distance education*, Oxford: Permagon, pp. 63–73.

Noble, D. (1998) 'The coming battle over online education', *Sociological Perspectives*, 41, 4: 815–818.

Noble, D. (ed.) (2002) *Digital diploma mills: The automation of higher education*, New York: Monthly Review Press.

Olson, D. K. (1994) *The world on paper: The conceptual and cognitive implications of reading and writing*, Cambridge and New York: Cambridge University Press.

Ong, W. (1982) *Orality and literacy*, New York: Routledge.

Palloff, R. and Pratt, K. (1999) *Building learning communities in Cyberspace*, San Francisco: Jossey-Bass.

Paul, R. (1990) *Critical thinking*, Rohnert Park: Sonoma State University.

Paulsen, M. (1995) 'Moderating Educational Computer Conferences', in Z. Berge and M. Collins (eds) *Computer mediated communication and the online classroom*, Cresskill, NJ: Hampton Press, Inc, pp. 81–90.

Peters, O. (1988) 'Distance teaching and industrial production: A comparative interpretation in outline', in D. Sewart, D. Keegan and B. Holmberg (eds) *Distance education: International perspectives*, London/New York: CroomHelm/St. Martin's Press, pp. 95–111.

Peters, O. (2000) 'Digital learning environments: New possibilities and opportunities', *International Review of Research in Open and Distance Learning*, 1, 1. Available [Online]: http://www.irrodl.org/content/v1.1/otto.pdf. Retrieved 6 June 2002.

Phipps, R. (2000) 'Measuring quality in Internet based higher education: Benchmarks for success', *International Higher Education*, 20, 2–4.

Pratt, D. D. (1981) 'The dynamics of continuing education learning groups', *Canadian Journal of University Continuing Education*, 8, 1: 26–32.

Privateer, P. M. (1999) 'Academic technology and the future of higher education', *The Journal of Higher Education*, 70, 1: 60–79.

Ramsden, P. (1988) 'Context and strategy: Situational influences on learning', in R. R. Schmeck (ed.) *Learning strategies and learning styles*, New York: Plenum, pp. 159–184.

Ramsden, P. (1992) *Learning to teach in higher education*, London: Routledge.

Report of a University of Illinois Faculty Seminar (1999) 'Teaching at an Internet distance: the pedagogy of online teaching and learning', Chicago: University of Illinois. Available [online]: http://www.vpaa.uillinois.edu/reports_retreats/tid_toc.asp. Retrieved 10 October 2002.

Report of the Web-Based Education Commission (2001) 'The power of the internet for learning: Moving from promise to practice', The President and the Congress of the United States. Available [Online]: http://interact.hpcnet.org/webcommission/index.htm. Retrieved 2 February 2002.

Resnick, L. B. (1987) *Education and learning to think*, Washington, DC: National Academy Press.

Resnick, L. B. (1991) 'Shared cognition: Thinking as social practice', in L. B. Resnick, J. M. Levine and S. D. Teasley (eds) *Perspective on socially shared cognition*, Washington, DC: American Psychological Association.

Resnick, M. (1996) 'Distributed constructivism', *Proceedings of the International Conference on the Learning Sciences Association for the Advancement of Computing in Education*, Northwestern University, Retrieved 6 June 2002. Available [Online]: http://el.www.media.mit.edu/groups/el/Papers/mres/Distrib-Construc/Distrib-Construc.html#RTFToC1. Retrieved 6 June 2002.

Rogoff, B. (1990) *Apprenticeship in thinking: Cognitive development in social context*, New York: Oxford University Press.

Rosenberg, M. J. (2001) *e-Learning: Strategies for delivering knowledge in the digital age*, New York: McGraw-Hill.

Rossman, M. (1999) 'Successful online teaching using an asynchronous learner discussion forum', *Journal of Asynchronous Learning Network*, 3, 2. Available [Online]: http://www.aln.org/alnweb/journal/Vol3_issue2/Rossman.htm.

Rourke, L. and Anderson, T. (2002) 'Using peer teams to lead online discussions', *Journal of Interactive Media in Education*, 2002: 1 ISSN:1365–893X [www-jime. open.ac.uk/2002/1].

Rourke, L. and Anderson, T. (in press) 'Exploring social communication in computer conferencing', *Internet Technologies, Applications and Issues*.

Rourke, L., Anderson, T., Archer, W. and Garrison, D. R. (1999) 'Assessing social presence in asynchronous, text-based computer conferences', *Journal of Distance Education*, 14, 3: 51–70.

Rourke, L., Anderson, T., Garrison, R. and Archer, W. (2001) 'Methodological issues in the content analysis of computer conference transcripts', *International Journal of Artificial Intelligence in Education*, 12, 1: 8–22. Available [Online]: http://www.atl.ualberta.ca/CMC.

Rowntree, D. (1977) *Assessing students*, London: Harper and Row.

Russell, T. L. (1999) 'The "no significant difference" phenomenon', *Research reports, summaries, and papers #248* (4th ed.), Raleigh, NC: North Carolina State University.

Schön, D. (1988) *Educating the reflective practitioner*, London: Jossey-Bass Publishers.

Schrage, M. (1989) *No more teams! Mastering the dynamics of creative collaboration*, New York: Currency Doubleday.

Seels, B. B. and Richey, R. C. (1994) *Instructional technology: The definition and domains of the field*, Washington, DC: Association for Educational Communications and Technology.

Senge, P. (1990) *The fifth discipline: The art and practice of the learning organization*, New York: Doubleday Publishers.

Short, J., Williams, E. and Christie, B. (1976) *The Social Psychology of Telecommunications*, Toronto: John Wiley and Sons.

Sims, R. (2001) 'From art to alchemy: Achieving success with online learning', *IT Forum*, 55. Available [Online]: http://it.coe.uga.edu/itforum/paper55.htm. Retrieved 6 June 2000.

Skinner, B. F. (1968) *The technology of teaching*, Englewood Cliffs, NJ: Prentice-Hall.

Stein, D. (1992) (ed.) *Cooperating with written texts: The pragmatics and comprehension of written texts*, Berlin & New York: Mouton de Gruyter.

Taylor, J. (2001) 'The future of learning – learning for the future: Shaping the transition', *Proceedings of the 20th ICDE World Congress*. Available [Online]: http://www.fernuni-hagen.de/ICDE/D-2001/final/keynote_speeches/wednesday/ taylor_keynote.pdf. Retrieved 6 June 2002.

Taylor, P. G. and Richardson, A. S. (2001) *Validating scholarship in university teaching: Constructing a national scheme for external peer review of ICT-based teaching and learning resources*. Available [Online]: http://www.detya.gov.au/ highered/eippubs/eip01_3/01_3.pdf.

Trochim, W. M. (2000) *The research methods knowledge base* (2nd ed.). Retrieved March 2002 from http://trochim.human.cornell.edu/kb/index.htm.

Tuckman, B. W. (1965) 'Developmental sequence in small groups', *Psychological Bulletin*, 63: 309–316.

Vassileva, J., Greer, J. M. G., Deters, R., Zapata, D., Mudgal, C. and Grant, S. (1999) 'A multi-agent approach to the design of peer-help environments', *Proceedings of AIED'99. Artificial Intelligence in Education*. Available [Online]: http://julita.usask.ca/homepage/Agents.htm.

Walther, J. (1992) 'Interpersonal effects in computer mediated interaction: A relational perspective', *Communication Research*, 19, 1: 52–90.

Wells, G. (1999) *Dialogic inquiry*, Cambridge: Cambridge University Press.

Wenger, E. (2001) *Supporting communities of practice: A survey of community-orientated technologies*, Shareware. Available [Online]: http://www.ewenger.com/tech/.

Winner, L. (1997) 'The handwriting on the wall: Resisting technoglobism's assault on education', in M. Moll (ed.) *Tech high: Globalization and the future of Canadian education*, Halifax: Fernwood Publishing, pp. 167–188.

Young, J. R. (1997) 'Rethinking the role of the professor in an age of high-tech tools', *The Chronicle of Higher Education*, 3 October: A26–A28.

Young, J. R. (2001) 'MIT begins effort to create public web pages for more than 2,000 of its courses', *The Chronicle of Higher Education*, 14 December: A34.

Zaiane, O. (2001) 'Web site mining for better web-based learning environments', in T. Calvert, and T. Keenan (eds) *Proceedings of computers and advanced technology in education conference*, Calgary: ACTA Press.

Zhu, E. (1996) *Meaning negotiation, knowledge construction, and mentoring in a distance learning course* (ERIC Document Reproduction Service, ED 397 849).

Index